Bread Inspired Recipes from Gordon Ramsay's Culinary Canvas

Exquisite Fusion Flavor Nook

Copyright © 2023 Exquisite Fusion Flavor Nook
All rights reserved.
:

Contents

INTRODUCTION 8
1. Classic French Baguette 10
2. Whole Wheat Sourdough 11
3. Rosemary Olive Oil Ciabatta 13
4. Cranberry Walnut Artisan Loaf 14
5. Garlic Parmesan Focaccia 16
6. Sun-dried Tomato Basil Bread 18
7. Pesto Swirl Bread 19
8. Cheddar and Chive Brioche 21
9. Seeded Multigrain Loaf 23
10. Caramelized Onion Rye Bread 25
11. Spicy Jalapeño Cornbread 26
12. Mediterranean Olive Bread 28
13. Sage and Brown Butter Pretzel Rolls 30
14. Fig and Goat Cheese Bread 31
15. Rustic Roasted Garlic Boule 33
16. Lemon Poppy Seed Zucchini Bread 35
17. Cinnamon Raisin Challah 36
18. Smoked Gouda and Bacon Bread 38
19. Pistachio and Orange Blossom Bread 40
20. Basil Pesto Parmesan Knots 41
21. Roasted Red Pepper and Asiago Bread 43
22. Maple Bacon Bourbon Bread 45
23. Hazelnut Chocolate Swirl Bread 46
24. Prosciutto and Rosemary Fougasse 48
25. Everything Bagel Bread 50
26. Blueberry Lemon Almond Loaf 52
27. Irish Soda Bread with Golden Raisins 53

28. Spinach and Feta Pull-Apart Bread 55
29. Buttermilk Honey Wheat Bread 57
30. Roquefort and Walnut Batard 58
31. Cranberry Orange Cinnamon Swirl Bread 60
32. Ancho Chili Chocolate Sourdough 62
33. Pumpkin Sage Dinner Rolls 63
34. Apricot Pistachio Challah 65
35. Asiago and Black Pepper Baguette 67
36. Spelt and Honey Boule 68
37. Sunflower Seed Rye Bread 70
38. Lemon Thyme Focaccia 71
39. Caramel Apple Cinnamon Bread 73
40. Smoked Salmon and Dill Bagels 74
41. Date and Walnut Raisin Bread 77
42. Roasted Garlic and Parmesan Sourdough 78
43. Cheddar Jalapeño Beer Bread 80
44. Olive and Herb Semolina Bread 81
45. Cranberry Pecan Rye Bread 83
46. Garlic Herb Pizza Dough 85
47. Roasted Beet and Goat Cheese Bread 87
48. Dark Chocolate Cherry Sourdough 88
49. Tomato Basil Parmesan Focaccia 90
50. Cinnamon Swirl Pumpkin Bread 92
51. Three Cheese Rosemary Baguette 94
52. Orange Cranberry Walnut Bread 95
53. Brown Butter Sage Pretzel Bites 97
54. Parmesan Black Pepper Grissini 99
55. Fig and Prosciutto Fougasse 101
56. Cardamom Orange Blossom Brioche 103

57. Stout and Cheddar Beer Bread 104

58. Sun-dried Tomato Pesto Bread 106

59. Hazelnut Espresso Chocolate Loaf 107

60. Caramelized Onion and Gruyere Boule 109

61. Lemon Herb Quinoa Bread 111

62. Roasted Garlic Parmesan Knots 112

63. Sweet Potato Sage Dinner Rolls 114

64. Raspberry Almond Bread 115

65. Asiago and Herb Sourdough 117

66. Pistachio Apricot Focaccia 118

67. Rosemary Sea Salt Bagels 120

68. Blue Cheese and Walnut Bread 122

69. Pumpkin Seed Spelt Bread 123

70. Orange Cranberry Pistachio Bread 125

71. Sage and Brown Butter Pretzel Buns 127

72. Cheddar Bacon Jalapeño Cornbread 129

73. Fig and Walnut Artisan Loaf 130

74. Cinnamon Raisin Walnut Challah 132

75. Garlic Parmesan Pizza Dough 134

76. Smoked Salmon and Dill Focaccia 136

77. Pesto Sunflower Seed Bread 137

78. Cranberry Orange Walnut Sourdough 139

79. Chive and Gouda Beer Bread 141

80. Sundried Tomato Basil Baguette 142

81. Caramelized Onion and Thyme Brioche 144

82. Walnut Rosemary Olive Bread 145

83. Roasted Red Pepper and Feta Bread 147

84. Pumpkin Sage Fougasse 149

85. Lemon Blueberry Almond Loaf 150

86. Cheddar Jalapeño Pretzel Rolls 152
87. Honey Wheat Sunflower Seed Bread 153
88. Prosciutto and Fig Baguette 155
89. Parmesan Garlic Herb Ciabatta 157
90. Apricot Almond Rye Bread 158
91. Basil Pesto Parmesan Fougasse 160
92. Dark Chocolate Cherry Challah 162
93. Sun-dried Tomato Basil Sourdough 164
94. Garlic Parmesan Rosemary Rolls 165
95. Fig and Goat Cheese Focaccia 167
96. Cranberry Orange Cinnamon Bread 169
97. Asiago and Black Pepper Boule 171
98. Sunflower Seed Rye Bagels 173
99. Lemon Thyme Olive Oil Bread 174
100. Cheddar Bacon Beer Bread 176
101. Rosemary Sea Salt Fougasse 177
102. Hazelnut Chocolate Swirl Brioche 179
103. Pesto Sun-dried Tomato Ciabatta 181
CONCLUSION 183

INTRODUCTION

Welcome to the culinary realm of Bread Bliss, a cookbook born from the passion for cooking and the relentless pursuit of gastronomic excellence inspired by the legendary Gordon Ramsay. In this delightful journey through the world of bread, we embark on a gastronomic adventure where the aromatic allure of freshly baked loaves meets Ramsay's signature flair for flavor.

Gordon Ramsay, a culinary maestro known for his prowess in the kitchen, has left an indelible mark on the culinary landscape with his innovative recipes and uncompromising standards. While he may not have delved extensively into the world of bread, his commitment to quality, bold flavors, and creative techniques has been a guiding light in the creation of this cookbook. As a passionate fan of Ramsay's work and an ardent devotee of the culinary arts, I present to you Bread Bliss, a collection of 103 bread machine recipes that encapsulate the essence of Gordon Ramsay's culinary philosophy.

The art of baking has always held a special place in the heart of every home cook. There's a therapeutic magic in the rhythmic kneading of dough, the transformation of simple ingredients into golden, crusty masterpieces, and the heavenly aroma that wafts through the kitchen. Bread, often referred to as the staff of life, becomes the canvas for Ramsay's influence in this cookbook. Each recipe is a testament to his dedication to culinary excellence and his belief in elevating the simplest ingredients to extraordinary heights.

In Bread Bliss, we explore the versatility of bread machines, demystifying the process and making the art of baking accessible to all, regardless of skill level. The recipes are crafted to reflect Ramsay's innovative spirit while ensuring that the joy of baking remains at the forefront. From artisanal loaves to unique flavored breads, the collection covers a spectrum of textures and tastes that will tantalize your taste buds and leave you yearning for more.

As we delve into the pages of this cookbook, you'll find a careful balance between Ramsay's bold, contemporary twists and the comforting nostalgia of traditional bread-making. The recipes are meticulously curated to offer a diverse selection, ensuring there's a perfect loaf for every occasion. Whether you're a seasoned baker looking to expand your repertoire or a novice eager to embark on a culinary adventure, Bread

Bliss provides a gateway to explore the delightful world of bread making.

Beyond the recipes, Bread Bliss aims to share the joy of the culinary journey, encouraging readers to embrace the art of cooking with passion and creativity. As we draw inspiration from Gordon Ramsay's culinary legacy, we also celebrate the joy that comes from crafting delicious, homemade bread that brings people together.

So, join me in this culinary odyssey, where the enticing aroma of freshly baked bread intertwines with the spirit of Gordon Ramsay's culinary magic. Let Bread Bliss be your companion in the kitchen as you create, savor, and share the joy of exceptional bread with your loved ones. Get ready to experience the ultimate bliss – the harmonious convergence of Gordon Ramsay's culinary influence and the soul-satisfying art of bread making.

1. Classic French Baguette

Indulge in the timeless charm of French baking with this Classic French Baguette recipe, a culinary masterpiece inspired by the renowned Gordon Ramsay. Elevate your bread machine experience as you embark on a journey to recreate the authentic taste and texture of a traditional French baguette. With a crisp golden crust and a soft, airy interior, this baguette is perfect for any occasion, whether paired with a savory cheese board or as the star of a sandwich.

Serving: Yields 2 baguettes
Preparation Time: 15 minutes
Ready Time: 2 hours 30 minutes

Ingredients:
- 1 1/2 cups warm water (110°F/43°C)
- 1 tablespoon sugar
- 2 teaspoons active dry yeast
- 4 cups bread flour
- 1 1/2 teaspoons salt
- Olive oil (for greasing)

Instructions:
1. In a small bowl, combine warm water and sugar. Stir until the sugar dissolves. Sprinkle the yeast over the water and let it sit for about 5 minutes, or until foamy.
2. In the bread machine pan, add the flour and make a well in the center. Pour the yeast mixture into the well.
3. Sprinkle the salt over the flour.
4. Set your bread machine to the "Dough" cycle and start the machine. Allow it to mix and knead the dough.
5. Once the dough cycle is complete, transfer the dough to a floured surface. Divide it into two equal portions.
6. Roll each portion into a long, thin rope, tapering the ends to create the classic baguette shape.
7. Place the shaped baguettes on a greased or parchment-lined baking sheet. Cover with a clean kitchen towel and let them rise in a warm place for about 45 minutes, or until doubled in size.

8. Preheat your oven to 450°F (230°C).
9. Using a sharp knife or razor blade, make diagonal slashes on the top of each baguette.
10. Bake in the preheated oven for 20-25 minutes or until the baguettes are golden brown and sound hollow when tapped on the bottom.
11. Allow the baguettes to cool on a wire rack before slicing.

Nutrition Information:
Note: Nutritional values are approximate and may vary based on specific ingredients and serving sizes.
- Calories per serving: 150
- Total Fat: 1g
- Cholesterol: 0mg
- Sodium: 300mg
- Total Carbohydrates: 30g
- Dietary Fiber: 1g
- Sugars: 1g
- Protein: 5g

Embrace the culinary magic of Gordon Ramsay with this Classic French Baguette recipe, a delightful addition to your repertoire of bread machine creations. Bon appétit!

2. Whole Wheat Sourdough

Elevate your bread-making game with this delectable Whole Wheat Sourdough recipe, inspired by the culinary genius of Gordon Ramsay. Sourdough bread, with its distinctive tangy flavor and chewy texture, gets a wholesome twist with the addition of whole wheat flour. Using a bread machine simplifies the process, allowing you to enjoy the rich aroma and taste of homemade sourdough with minimal effort.

Serving: Makes one hearty loaf of Whole Wheat Sourdough.
Preparation Time: 15 minutes (plus additional time for sourdough starter)
Ready Time: Approximately 24-48 hours (including fermentation and baking time)

Ingredients:

- 1 cup active sourdough starter
- 2 cups whole wheat flour
- 2 cups bread flour
- 1 ½ teaspoons salt
- 1 ½ cups lukewarm water

Instructions:
1. Prepare the Sourdough Starter:
If you don't have an active sourdough starter, combine equal parts whole wheat flour and water in a glass container. Stir well and let it sit, loosely covered, at room temperature. Feed the starter with equal parts flour and water daily until it becomes bubbly and doubles in size (usually takes about 5-7 days).
2. Mixing the Dough:
In the bread machine pan, combine the active sourdough starter, whole wheat flour, bread flour, and salt. Add lukewarm water. Place the pan in the bread machine.
3. Kneading and Rising:
Set the bread machine to the dough setting and let it knead and rise. This typically takes about 1.5 to 2 hours, depending on your machine.
4. Shaping and Final Rise:
Once the dough cycle is complete, remove the dough from the machine and shape it into a round loaf. Place the shaped dough on a floured surface, cover it with a clean kitchen towel, and let it rise for an additional 6-12 hours, or until doubled in size.
5. Baking:
Preheat the oven to 450°F (230°C). Place a Dutch oven or baking pot in the oven to heat. Once hot, carefully transfer the risen dough into the preheated pot. Cover and bake for 30 minutes. Remove the lid and bake for an additional 15-20 minutes or until the crust is golden brown.
6. Cooling:
Allow the sourdough to cool on a wire rack before slicing. Enjoy slices spread with butter or your favorite toppings!

Nutrition Information:
Note: Nutritional values are approximate and may vary based on specific ingredients and serving size.
- Calories per serving: XXX
- Total Fat: XXg
- Saturated Fat: XXg

- Cholesterol: XXmg
- Sodium: XXXmg
- Total Carbohydrates: XXg
- Dietary Fiber: XXg
- Sugars: XXg
- Protein: XXg

Now, savor the satisfaction of creating a delightful Whole Wheat Sourdough loaf, embodying the essence of artisanal bread with the convenience of a bread machine.

3. Rosemary Olive Oil Ciabatta

Elevate your bread machine experience with this delectable Rosemary Olive Oil Ciabatta, a recipe inspired by the culinary genius of Gordon Ramsay. This artisanal bread combines the fragrant essence of rosemary with the richness of olive oil, resulting in a delightful flavor that pairs perfectly with a variety of dishes. The ease of preparation in your bread machine makes this recipe a must-try for both beginners and seasoned bakers.

Serving: Yields 1 loaf, approximately 10 slices.
Preparation Time: 15 minutes
Ready Time: 3 hours (includes rise time)

Ingredients:
- 1 cup warm water
- 2 tablespoons olive oil
- 1 teaspoon sugar
- 1 teaspoon salt
- 3 cups bread flour
- 1 1/2 teaspoons active dry yeast
- 1 tablespoon fresh rosemary, finely chopped
- 1/2 cup Kalamata olives, pitted and chopped

Instructions:
1. In the bread machine pan, combine warm water, olive oil, sugar, and salt.
2. Add bread flour to the pan, creating an even layer.

3. Make a well in the center of the flour and add the active dry yeast.
4. Sprinkle the finely chopped rosemary over the flour.
5. Start the bread machine on the dough cycle. If your machine has an option for adding ingredients, add the Kalamata olives when prompted or during the last 5 minutes of the kneading cycle.
6. Once the dough cycle is complete, transfer the dough to a lightly floured surface and shape it into an oval or rectangular loaf.
7. Place the shaped dough on a parchment-lined baking sheet, cover with a clean kitchen towel, and let it rise in a warm place for about 1-2 hours, or until it doubles in size.
8. Preheat the oven to 400°F (200°C). Optionally, you can place a small pan of water on the bottom rack of the oven to create steam, which helps achieve a crisp crust.
9. Bake the ciabatta for 20-25 minutes or until it is golden brown and sounds hollow when tapped on the bottom.
10. Allow the bread to cool on a wire rack before slicing and serving.

Nutrition Information:
Note: Nutritional values are approximate and may vary based on specific ingredients and serving sizes.
- Calories per serving: 180
- Total Fat: 6g
- Saturated Fat: 1g
- Trans Fat: 0g
- Cholesterol: 0mg
- Sodium: 290mg
- Total Carbohydrates: 28g
- Dietary Fiber: 2g
- Sugars: 0.5g
- Protein: 5g

4. Cranberry Walnut Artisan Loaf

Elevate your bread machine experience with this Cranberry Walnut Artisan Loaf inspired by the culinary genius, Gordon Ramsay. Bursting with the sweet-tart flavor of cranberries and the rich crunch of walnuts, this bread is a delightful combination of textures and tastes. The aroma that fills your kitchen as it bakes is as irresistible as the loaf itself. Get ready to impress your taste buds and those of your guests with this artisanal creation!

Serving: Makes one 1.5 lb loaf, approximately 12 slices.
Preparation Time: 15 minutes
Ready Time: 3 hours (including rise and bake time)

Ingredients:
- 1 cup warm water (110°F/43°C)
- 2 tablespoons olive oil
- 3 cups bread flour
- 1 teaspoon salt
- 2 tablespoons sugar
- 1.5 teaspoons active dry yeast
- 1/2 cup dried cranberries
- 1/2 cup chopped walnuts

Instructions:
1. Prep the Machine:
- Place the warm water and olive oil in the bread machine pan.
2. Add Dry Ingredients:
- In a separate bowl, mix the bread flour, salt, and sugar. Add this mixture to the bread machine pan.
3. Create a Well:
- Make a well in the center of the dry ingredients and add the active dry yeast.
4. Start the Machine:
- Set your bread machine to the "Basic" or "White Bread" setting, depending on your machine model.
5. Incorporate Mix-ins:
- When the machine signals for mix-ins (usually after the first kneading cycle), add the dried cranberries and chopped walnuts.
6. Monitor the Dough:
- Keep an eye on the dough consistency during the initial mixing. If it seems too sticky, add a tablespoon of flour at a time until a smooth ball forms.
7. Let it Rise:
- Allow the bread machine to complete its cycle, including the rising time.
8. Preheat and Bake:

- Preheat your oven to 350°F (175°C) during the last 15 minutes of the final rise. Once the machine signals the end of the cycle, transfer the dough to a greased or parchment-lined baking sheet and bake in the preheated oven for 25-30 minutes or until the loaf is golden brown.

9. Cool and Slice:
- Allow the Cranberry Walnut Artisan Loaf to cool on a wire rack before slicing.

Nutrition Information:
- Serving Size: 1 slice
- Calories: 150
- Total Fat: 5g
- Saturated Fat: 1g
- Cholesterol: 0mg
- Sodium: 150mg
- Total Carbohydrates: 24g
- Dietary Fiber: 2g
- Sugars: 4g
- Protein: 4g

Enjoy this Cranberry Walnut Artisan Loaf with your favorite spreads or as a flavorful accompaniment to soups and salads. Gordon Ramsay would undoubtedly approve of this delightful creation from your own kitchen!

5. Garlic Parmesan Focaccia

Elevate your bread machine game with this irresistible Garlic Parmesan Focaccia inspired by the culinary genius of Gordon Ramsay. The aromatic blend of garlic and Parmesan cheese perfectly complements the light, fluffy texture of this classic Italian bread. With the convenience of a bread machine, you'll achieve bakery-quality results in the comfort of your own kitchen.

Serving: Makes one 9x13-inch focaccia, serving 12
Preparation Time: 15 minutes
Ready Time: 2 hours 30 minutes (includes rising time)

Ingredients:

- 1 1/2 cups warm water (110°F/43°C)
- 2 tablespoons olive oil
- 4 cups bread flour
- 1 teaspoon sugar
- 1 1/2 teaspoons salt
- 2 teaspoons active dry yeast

For Topping:
- 1/4 cup olive oil
- 4 cloves garlic, minced
- 1/4 cup grated Parmesan cheese
- 1 tablespoon fresh rosemary, finely chopped
- Sea salt, to taste

Instructions:
1. Place the warm water, olive oil, bread flour, sugar, salt, and active dry yeast into the bread machine pan in the order recommended by the manufacturer.
2. Select the "Dough" cycle on your bread machine and press start. Allow the machine to complete the cycle, including the first rise.
3. Once the dough cycle is complete, transfer the risen dough to a lightly floured surface. Preheat your oven to 375°F (190°C).
4. Roll out the dough to fit a greased 9x13-inch baking pan. Place the rolled-out dough into the pan and press it down to fill the corners.
5. In a small bowl, mix together the olive oil and minced garlic. Brush the garlic-infused oil over the surface of the dough.
6. Sprinkle the grated Parmesan cheese evenly over the dough, followed by the chopped rosemary. Finish by sprinkling a touch of sea salt over the top.
7. Allow the dough to rise for an additional 30 minutes in a warm place.
8. Bake in the preheated oven for 20-25 minutes or until the focaccia is golden brown and sounds hollow when tapped on the bottom.
9. Remove from the oven and let it cool in the pan for 5 minutes before transferring to a wire rack to cool completely.

Nutrition Information (per serving):
- Calories: 230
- Total Fat: 8g
- Saturated Fat: 1.5g
- Cholesterol: 2mg
- Sodium: 330mg

- Total Carbohydrates: 32g
- Dietary Fiber: 2g
- Sugars: 0.5g
- Protein: 6g

Indulge in the rich flavors of this Garlic Parmesan Focaccia, a delightful creation that will impress even the most discerning palate. Enjoy it as a standalone treat or alongside your favorite soups and salads.

6. Sun-dried Tomato Basil Bread

Elevate your bread machine experience with this delightful Sun-dried Tomato Basil Bread, inspired by the culinary genius of Gordon Ramsay. Infused with the rich flavors of sun-dried tomatoes and aromatic basil, this bread is a perfect blend of savory goodness. Your kitchen will be filled with the irresistible aroma as this bread bakes to perfection. Serve it warm with butter or use it to make gourmet sandwiches - either way, you're in for a treat!

Serving: Makes one loaf (approximately 12 slices).
Preparation Time: 15 minutes
Ready Time: 3 hours (including rising and baking time)

Ingredients:
- 1 cup warm water (110°F/43°C)
- 2 tablespoons olive oil
- 1 teaspoon sugar
- 1 1/2 teaspoons salt
- 3 cups bread flour
- 1/4 cup finely chopped sun-dried tomatoes (packed in oil, drained)
- 2 tablespoons fresh basil, chopped
- 1 1/2 teaspoons active dry yeast

Instructions:
1. In the bread machine pan, combine warm water, olive oil, sugar, and salt.
2. Add the bread flour to the pan, creating a well in the center.
3. Sprinkle the chopped sun-dried tomatoes and fresh basil into the well.
4. In a small indentation on top of the flour, add the active dry yeast.

5. Place the pan in the bread machine and select the "Basic" or "White Bread" setting with a medium crust.
6. Start the machine, allowing it to mix, knead, rise, and bake the bread according to the manufacturer's instructions.
7. Once the baking cycle is complete, carefully remove the bread from the machine and transfer it to a wire rack to cool.

Nutrition Information:
(Per slice, based on 12 slices)
- Calories: 150
- Total Fat: 3.5g
- Saturated Fat: 0.5g
- Trans Fat: 0g
- Cholesterol: 0mg
- Sodium: 300mg
- Total Carbohydrates: 25g
- Dietary Fiber: 1g
- Sugars: 1g
- Protein: 4g

Enjoy the Sun-dried Tomato Basil Bread as a standalone delight or use it to bring a gourmet twist to your sandwiches. Embrace the culinary inspiration of Gordon Ramsay right in your own kitchen!

7. Pesto Swirl Bread

Elevate your bread machine game with this delightful Pesto Swirl Bread inspired by the culinary genius, Gordon Ramsay. The aromatic blend of fresh basil, garlic, pine nuts, and Parmesan cheese creates a flavorful pesto that swirls through the soft, golden strands of bread, making it a feast for the senses. Perfect for any occasion, this bread will not only satisfy your taste buds but also fill your kitchen with the irresistible aroma of a professional bakery.

Serving: Serves: 8-10 slices
Preparation Time: 15 minutes
Ready Time: 3 hours

Ingredients:

- 1 cup warm water (110°F/43°C)
- 2 tablespoons olive oil
- 3 cups bread flour
- 1 teaspoon sugar
- 1 teaspoon salt
- 2 teaspoons active dry yeast
- Pesto Filling:
- 2 cups fresh basil leaves, packed
- 3 cloves garlic
- 1/2 cup pine nuts
- 1/2 cup grated Parmesan cheese
- 1/2 cup olive oil
- Salt and pepper to taste

Instructions:
1. Prepare Pesto Filling:
a. In a food processor, combine fresh basil, garlic, pine nuts, and Parmesan cheese.
b. Pulse until ingredients are finely chopped.
c. With the processor running, slowly drizzle in the olive oil until a smooth pesto consistency is achieved.
d. Season with salt and pepper to taste. Set aside.
2. Prepare Bread Dough:
a. In the bread machine pan, combine warm water and olive oil.
b. In a separate bowl, whisk together bread flour, sugar, and salt.
c. Add the dry ingredients to the bread machine pan, creating a well in the center.
d. Place yeast in the well. Follow your bread machine's instructions for the order of adding ingredients.
3. Select Dough Setting:
a. Choose the dough setting on your bread machine and start the cycle.
4. Roll Out Dough:
a. Once the dough cycle is complete, transfer the dough to a floured surface.
b. Roll out the dough into a rectangle, approximately 12x18 inches.
5. Spread Pesto:
a. Evenly spread the prepared pesto over the rolled-out dough, leaving a small border around the edges.
6. Roll the Dough:

a. Starting from one of the longer sides, carefully roll the dough into a log.
7. Shape the Bread:
a. Place the rolled dough into a greased loaf pan, ensuring the seam side is facing down.
8. Final Rise:
a. Cover the loaf pan with a clean kitchen towel and let the dough rise for an additional 30-45 minutes, or until it has doubled in size.
9. Bake:
a. Preheat your oven to 375°F (190°C).
b. Bake the bread for 25-30 minutes or until golden brown on top.
10. Cool and Slice:
a. Allow the bread to cool in the pan for 10 minutes before transferring it to a wire rack to cool completely.
b. Once cooled, slice and serve.

Nutrition Information (per serving):
- Calories: 280
- Total Fat: 16g
- Saturated Fat: 3g
- Cholesterol: 5mg
- Sodium: 350mg
- Total Carbohydrates: 28g
- Dietary Fiber: 2g
- Sugars: 1g
- Protein: 6g

Enjoy this Pesto Swirl Bread as a delectable accompaniment to any meal or as a stand-alone treat. Your taste buds will thank you for the burst of flavors in every bite!

8. Cheddar and Chive Brioche

Elevate your bread machine experience with the delectable fusion of rich cheddar and the aromatic essence of chives in this Cheddar and Chive Brioche. Inspired by the culinary genius of Gordon Ramsay, this recipe promises a delightful twist to the classic brioche, marrying flavors that will leave your taste buds dancing. The bread machine makes the process a breeze, ensuring a soft, cheesy, and flavorful loaf that's perfect for any occasion.

Serving: Makes one 1.5-pound loaf, approximately 12 slices.
Preparation Time: 15 minutes
Ready Time: 3 hours (including rising and baking time)

Ingredients:
- 1 cup milk, lukewarm
- 3 large eggs
- 1/4 cup unsalted butter, softened
- 4 cups bread flour
- 1/4 cup sugar
- 1 teaspoon salt
- 1 1/2 teaspoons active dry yeast
- 1 cup sharp cheddar cheese, shredded
- 1/4 cup fresh chives, finely chopped

Instructions:
1. Prepare the Bread Machine:
Place the milk, eggs, and butter into the bread machine pan.
2. Add Dry Ingredients:
In a separate bowl, whisk together the bread flour, sugar, and salt. Add this mixture on top of the wet ingredients in the bread machine pan, creating a barrier for the yeast.
3. Create a Well for Yeast:
Make a small well in the center of the flour mixture and add the active dry yeast.
4. Start the Machine:
Insert the bread machine pan into the machine and select the "Dough" or "Manual" setting. Start the machine, allowing it to mix and knead the ingredients until a soft dough forms.
5. Incorporate Cheese and Chives:
Once the dough is ready, add the shredded cheddar cheese and chopped chives. Allow the machine to continue kneading until the cheese and chives are evenly distributed throughout the dough.
6. First Rise:
Leave the dough in the machine for the first rise, following the machine's instructions.
7. Shape the Brioche:

After the first rise, remove the dough and shape it into a loaf. Place it in a greased 9x5-inch loaf pan.

8. Second Rise:

Cover the pan with a clean kitchen towel and let the dough rise again until it doubles in size, approximately 1-1.5 hours.

9. Bake:

Preheat your oven to 350°F (175°C). Bake the brioche for 25-30 minutes or until the top is golden brown and the loaf sounds hollow when tapped.

10. Cool and Enjoy:

Allow the Cheddar and Chive Brioche to cool in the pan for 10 minutes before transferring it to a wire rack to cool completely. Slice and enjoy!

Nutrition Information:

Note: Nutritional values are approximate and may vary based on specific ingredients used.
- Serving Size: 1 slice
- Calories: 220
- Total Fat: 9g
- Saturated Fat: 5g
- Cholesterol: 60mg
- Sodium: 230mg
- Total Carbohydrates: 27g
- Dietary Fiber: 1g
- Sugars: 3g
- Protein: 8g

Feel free to adjust the serving size and ingredient quantities based on your preferences and dietary needs. Enjoy your homemade Cheddar and Chive Brioche!

9. Seeded Multigrain Loaf

Elevate your bread-making game with this Seeded Multigrain Loaf, a wholesome creation inspired by the culinary genius of Gordon Ramsay. Packed with a variety of seeds and grains, this bread is not only delicious but also a nutritional powerhouse. Let the aroma of freshly baked goodness fill your kitchen as you master the art of crafting this exceptional loaf using your bread machine.

Serving: Makes one large loaf, approximately 12 slices.
Preparation Time: 15 minutes
Ready Time: 3 hours and 30 minutes

Ingredients:
- 1 cup warm water (110°F/43°C)
- 2 tablespoons honey
- 2 tablespoons olive oil
- 1 teaspoon salt
- 1 cup whole wheat flour
- 1 cup bread flour
- 1/2 cup rolled oats
- 1/4 cup flaxseeds
- 1/4 cup sunflower seeds
- 1/4 cup pumpkin seeds
- 2 tablespoons chia seeds
- 1 tablespoon sesame seeds
- 2 teaspoons active dry yeast

Instructions:
1. In the bread machine pan, combine warm water, honey, olive oil, and salt.
2. Add whole wheat flour, bread flour, rolled oats, flaxseeds, sunflower seeds, pumpkin seeds, chia seeds, sesame seeds, and active dry yeast.
3. Place the pan in the bread machine and select the whole grain or multigrain setting. Choose a medium crust setting.
4. Start the bread machine, and let it work its magic. Allow the machine to knead, rise, and bake the dough according to the selected setting.
5. Once the baking cycle is complete, carefully remove the hot bread from the machine and transfer it to a wire rack to cool completely.
6. Slice and serve this Seeded Multigrain Loaf with your favorite spreads or enjoy it on its own.

Nutrition Information:
(Per serving - 1 slice)
- Calories: 150
- Total Fat: 6g
- Saturated Fat: 1g
- Trans Fat: 0g

- Cholesterol: 0mg
- Sodium: 200mg
- Total Carbohydrates: 21g
- Dietary Fiber: 3g
- Sugars: 3g
- Protein: 4g

Indulge in the rich flavors and textures of this Seeded Multigrain Loaf, and impress your taste buds with every bite. A delightful addition to any meal, this bread is not only a treat for your senses but also a celebration of wholesome ingredients.

10. Caramelized Onion Rye Bread

Elevate your bread machine experience with the rich and savory flavors of Caramelized Onion Rye Bread, a recipe inspired by the culinary genius of Gordon Ramsay. This unique bread combines the earthy taste of rye with the sweet and savory notes of caramelized onions, resulting in a loaf that's perfect for sandwiches, toasting, or enjoying on its own. Follow the simple instructions below to bring a touch of gourmet flair to your home baking.

Serving: Makes one loaf (approximately 12 slices)
Preparation Time: 15 minutes
Ready Time: 3 hours and 30 minutes (including rising and baking time)

Ingredients:
- 1 large onion, thinly sliced
- 2 tablespoons olive oil
- 1 cup warm water
- 1 1/2 teaspoons salt
- 2 tablespoons honey
- 1 1/2 cups bread flour
- 1 1/2 cups rye flour
- 1 tablespoon caraway seeds (optional)
- 2 teaspoons active dry yeast

Instructions:

1. In a skillet over medium heat, sauté the thinly sliced onion in olive oil until golden brown and caramelized. Set aside to cool.
2. In the bread machine pan, combine warm water, salt, honey, bread flour, rye flour, and caraway seeds (if using).
3. Make a well in the center of the dry ingredients and add the active dry yeast. Place the caramelized onions on top.
4. Insert the bread machine pan into the machine and select the "Basic" or "Whole Wheat" setting, depending on your machine's options. Choose a medium crust setting.
5. Start the machine and let it run through the cycle. The aroma of caramelized onions and rye will fill your kitchen as the bread bakes to golden perfection.
6. Once the cycle is complete, carefully remove the bread from the machine and let it cool on a wire rack before slicing.

Nutrition Information (per slice):
- Calories: 120
- Total Fat: 3g
- Saturated Fat: 0.5g
- Cholesterol: 0mg
- Sodium: 250mg
- Total Carbohydrates: 21g
- Dietary Fiber: 2g
- Sugars: 2g
- Protein: 3g

Enjoy the delightful combination of sweet caramelized onions and hearty rye in every slice of this Gordon Ramsay-inspired masterpiece. Perfect for any occasion, this bread will become a staple in your home baking repertoire.

11. Spicy Jalapeño Cornbread

Elevate your bread machine repertoire with a kick of flavor inspired by the bold culinary style of Gordon Ramsay. This Spicy Jalapeño Cornbread recipe is a delightful fusion of warmth and heat, perfect for those who appreciate a bit of spice in their bread. The cornbread's golden exterior hides a moist and flavorful interior, making it an ideal accompaniment to soups, stews, or enjoyed on its own. Gordon

Ramsay's influence shines through in the harmonious blend of ingredients that create a memorable culinary experience.

Serving: Makes one 8-inch square pan of cornbread, approximately 9 servings.
Preparation Time: 15 minutes
Ready Time: 2 hours (including machine and baking time)

Ingredients:
- 1 cup yellow cornmeal
- 1 cup all-purpose flour
- 1 tablespoon baking powder
- 1/2 teaspoon baking soda
- 1/2 teaspoon salt
- 1 cup buttermilk
- 1/2 cup unsalted butter, melted
- 2 large eggs
- 1 cup shredded sharp cheddar cheese
- 1/4 cup chopped pickled jalapeños (adjust to taste)
- 1/4 cup chopped fresh cilantro

Instructions:
1. Place the yellow cornmeal, all-purpose flour, baking powder, baking soda, and salt in the bread machine pan.
2. In a separate bowl, whisk together the buttermilk, melted butter, and eggs.
3. Pour the wet ingredients into the bread machine pan over the dry ingredients.
4. Set the bread machine to the "Quick Bread" or "Cake" cycle, depending on your machine's options.
5. Add the shredded cheddar cheese, chopped jalapeños, and cilantro when prompted by your bread machine to add mix-ins (usually during the last few minutes of mixing).
6. Once the cycle is complete, carefully remove the bread pan from the machine.
7. Preheat your oven to 350°F (175°C).
8. Transfer the batter into a greased 8-inch square baking pan.
9. Bake for 25-30 minutes or until a toothpick inserted into the center comes out clean.

10. Allow the cornbread to cool in the pan for 10 minutes before transferring it to a wire rack to cool completely.

Nutrition Information (per serving):
- Calories: 280
- Total Fat: 16g
- Saturated Fat: 9g
- Trans Fat: 0g
- Cholesterol: 75mg
- Sodium: 460mg
- Total Carbohydrates: 25g
- Dietary Fiber: 2g
- Sugars: 2g
- Protein: 8g

Note: Nutrition information is approximate and may vary based on specific ingredients used. Adjust quantities and ingredients according to dietary preferences and restrictions.

12. Mediterranean Olive Bread

Experience the sun-soaked flavors of the Mediterranean with this delightful Olive Bread inspired by the culinary genius of Gordon Ramsay. This aromatic and savory bread, infused with the essence of olives, brings the warmth of the Mediterranean right to your kitchen. Created for bread machines, this recipe ensures that you can enjoy the delicious results with minimal effort. Perfect for a cozy family dinner or as a complement to your favorite dishes, this Mediterranean Olive Bread is a testament to the simplicity and sophistication of Gordon Ramsay's culinary style.

Serving: 1 loaf, approximately 12 slices
Preparation Time: 15 minutes
Ready Time: 3 hours and 15 minutes

Ingredients:
- 1 cup warm water
- 2 tablespoons olive oil
- 3 cups bread flour

- 1 teaspoon sugar
- 1 1/2 teaspoons salt
- 1 teaspoon dried oregano
- 1 teaspoon dried basil
- 1 teaspoon dried thyme
- 1 teaspoon garlic powder
- 1 1/2 teaspoons active dry yeast
- 1 cup pitted and chopped Kalamata olives
- 1/2 cup crumbled feta cheese

Instructions:
1. Place the warm water and olive oil into the bread machine pan.
2. In a separate bowl, combine the bread flour, sugar, salt, oregano, basil, thyme, and garlic powder. Mix well.
3. Add the dry ingredients to the bread machine pan on top of the water and oil.
4. Make a small well in the center of the dry ingredients and add the active dry yeast.
5. Select the "Dough" or "Pizza Dough" setting on your bread machine and start the cycle.
6. When the machine signals that the dough is ready, carefully remove it from the machine and place it on a lightly floured surface.
7. Preheat your oven to 375°F (190°C).
8. Flatten the dough into a rectangle and evenly distribute the chopped olives and crumbled feta cheese over the surface.
9. Roll the dough into a log, sealing the edges.
10. Place the shaped dough into a greased bread pan, cover with a clean kitchen towel, and let it rise for about 1 hour or until it has doubled in size.
11. Bake in the preheated oven for 25-30 minutes or until the bread has a golden-brown crust.
12. Allow the bread to cool for a few minutes before transferring it to a wire rack to cool completely.

Nutrition Information (per serving):
- Calories: 180
- Total Fat: 6g
- Saturated Fat: 2g
- Cholesterol: 6mg
- Sodium: 370mg

- Total Carbohydrates: 25g
- Dietary Fiber: 2g
- Sugars: 1g
- Protein: 6g

Enjoy this Mediterranean Olive Bread with a drizzle of olive oil, balsamic vinegar, or as a side to your favorite Mediterranean-inspired dishes. The combination of olives and feta creates a harmonious blend of flavors that will transport your taste buds to the azure shores of the Mediterranean.

13. Sage and Brown Butter Pretzel Rolls

Elevate your bread machine game with these delectable Sage and Brown Butter Pretzel Rolls inspired by the culinary genius, Gordon Ramsay. The perfect blend of earthy sage and rich brown butter takes traditional pretzel rolls to new heights. Soft on the inside with a golden-brown, slightly crisp exterior, these rolls are a testament to the art of bread-making. Follow this recipe to bring a touch of gourmet flair to your home kitchen.

Serving: Makes 12 pretzel rolls
Preparation Time: 20 minutes
Ready Time: 2 hours 30 minutes (including rising time)

Ingredients:
- 1 1/2 cups warm water (110°F/43°C)
- 1 tablespoon sugar
- 2 teaspoons active dry yeast
- 4 cups all-purpose flour
- 1 teaspoon salt
- 1/4 cup unsalted butter, melted
- 2 tablespoons chopped fresh sage
- 1/4 cup baking soda
- Coarse salt, for sprinkling

Instructions:
1. In a small bowl, combine warm water and sugar. Stir until sugar dissolves. Sprinkle yeast over the water and let it sit for about 5 minutes, or until foamy.

2. In the bread machine pan, add the flour, salt, melted butter, and activated yeast mixture. Select the dough cycle and start the machine.
3. Once the dough cycle is complete, transfer the dough to a lightly floured surface. Divide it into 12 equal portions and shape each into a ball.
4. In a saucepan over medium heat, melt additional 2 tablespoons of butter. Add chopped sage and cook until the butter turns golden brown and the sage becomes fragrant. Remove from heat.
5. Preheat your oven to 425°F (220°C).
6. In a large pot, bring water to a boil. Add baking soda and reduce to a simmer. Gently place each dough ball into the simmering water for 30 seconds, then transfer to a parchment-lined baking sheet.
7. Brush the rolls with the brown butter and sage mixture. Sprinkle coarse salt on top.
8. Bake in the preheated oven for 12-15 minutes, or until the rolls are golden brown.
9. Allow the rolls to cool for a few minutes before serving.

Nutrition Information:
(Per serving - 1 pretzel roll)
- Calories: 180
- Total Fat: 4g
- Saturated Fat: 2.5g
- Cholesterol: 10mg
- Sodium: 600mg
- Total Carbohydrates: 30g
- Dietary Fiber: 1g
- Sugars: 1g
- Protein: 5g

Enjoy these Sage and Brown Butter Pretzel Rolls as a delightful accompaniment to soups, sandwiches, or on their own for a gourmet bread experience at home!

14. Fig and Goat Cheese Bread

Indulge your taste buds in the sublime combination of sweet figs and rich goat cheese with this delectable Fig and Goat Cheese Bread. Inspired by Gordon Ramsay's culinary finesse, this bread machine recipe promises a delightful harmony of flavors and textures. Whether enjoyed as a standalone treat or paired with your favorite dishes, this bread is a testament to the art of baking elevated to new heights.

Serving: 12 slices
Preparation Time: 15 minutes
Ready Time: 3 hours and 15 minutes

Ingredients:
- 1 cup warm water (110°F/43°C)
- 2 tablespoons olive oil
- 3 cups bread flour
- 1 teaspoon salt
- 2 tablespoons honey
- 1 packet (2 1/4 teaspoons) active dry yeast
- 1/2 cup dried figs, chopped
- 1/2 cup goat cheese, crumbled
- 1 tablespoon fresh rosemary, chopped (optional, for added aroma)

Instructions:
1. Place the warm water, olive oil, bread flour, salt, honey, and active dry yeast in the bread machine pan, following the manufacturer's recommended order for ingredients.
2. Select the "Dough" or "Basic" setting on your bread machine and start the cycle. Allow the machine to knead and rise the dough, creating the perfect foundation for your bread.
3. Once the dough cycle is complete, gently remove the dough from the machine and place it on a floured surface. Press the chopped figs, crumbled goat cheese, and fresh rosemary (if using) evenly into the dough.
4. Shape the dough into a loaf and transfer it to a greased loaf pan. Cover the pan with a clean kitchen towel and let the dough rise in a warm place for about 1 to 1.5 hours, or until it has doubled in size.
5. Preheat your oven to 375°F (190°C). Bake the bread for 25-30 minutes, or until the top is golden brown, and the bread sounds hollow when tapped.
6. Allow the Fig and Goat Cheese Bread to cool in the pan for 10 minutes before transferring it to a wire rack to cool completely.

Nutrition Information (per slice):

- Calories: 180
- Total Fat: 5g
- Saturated Fat: 2g
- Cholesterol: 5mg
- Sodium: 210mg
- Total Carbohydrates: 30g
- Dietary Fiber: 2g
- Sugars: 6g
- Protein: 6g

Enjoy the delightful combination of sweet figs and savory goat cheese in every slice of this artisanal bread, creating a memorable culinary experience inspired by the renowned Gordon Ramsay.

15. Rustic Roasted Garlic Boule

Indulge your senses in the rich aroma and robust flavors of our Rustic Roasted Garlic Boule, a delightful bread machine creation inspired by the culinary genius of Gordon Ramsay. This artisanal loaf combines the simplicity of a bread machine with the elevated taste of roasted garlic, creating a perfect harmony of rustic charm and gourmet sophistication.

Serving: Makes one round loaf, perfect for sharing with friends and family.
Preparation Time: 15 minutes
Ready Time: 3 hours

Ingredients:
- 1 cup warm water (110°F/43°C)
- 2 tablespoons olive oil
- 1 1/2 teaspoons salt
- 1 teaspoon sugar
- 3 cups bread flour
- 2 teaspoons active dry yeast
- 1 head of garlic
- 2 tablespoons olive oil (for garlic roasting)

Instructions:
1. Prepare the Bread Machine:

- Place the warm water, olive oil, salt, sugar, bread flour, and active dry yeast into the bread machine pan in the order recommended by the manufacturer.

2. Set the Bread Machine:
- Choose the appropriate setting for a basic white bread or a French bread cycle, depending on your machine. Start the machine.

3. Roast the Garlic:
- Preheat your oven to 400°F (200°C).
- Cut the top off the garlic head to expose the cloves.
- Place the garlic head on a piece of foil, drizzle with 2 tablespoons of olive oil, and wrap it in the foil.
- Roast in the preheated oven for 30-40 minutes or until the garlic cloves are soft and golden. Allow it to cool.

4. Add Roasted Garlic:
- Squeeze the roasted garlic cloves into a paste and fold it into the bread dough after the first rise. Knead lightly to distribute the garlic evenly.

5. Shape the Boule:
- Once the bread machine cycle is complete, remove the dough and shape it into a round boule. Place it on a parchment-lined baking sheet.

6. Final Rise:
- Allow the shaped dough to rise for an additional 30-45 minutes, or until it doubles in size.

7. Preheat the Oven:
- Preheat your oven to 375°F (190°C).

8. Bake:
- Bake the boule in the preheated oven for 25-30 minutes, or until the crust is golden brown and the bread sounds hollow when tapped.

9. Cool:
- Allow the Rustic Roasted Garlic Boule to cool on a wire rack before slicing.

Nutrition Information:
Note: Nutrition information is approximate and may vary based on specific ingredients used.
- Serving Size: 1 slice
- Calories: 120
- Total Fat: 4g
- Saturated Fat: 0.5g
- Cholesterol: 0mg
- Sodium: 230mg

- Total Carbohydrates: 18g
- Dietary Fiber: 1g
- Sugars: 0g
- Protein: 3g

Enjoy the irresistible allure of this Rustic Roasted Garlic Boule, a testament to the magic that happens when the convenience of a bread machine meets the culinary brilliance of Gordon Ramsay.

16. Lemon Poppy Seed Zucchini Bread

Elevate your bread machine repertoire with this delightful Lemon Poppy Seed Zucchini Bread—a harmonious blend of zesty lemon, nutty poppy seeds, and the subtle sweetness of zucchini. Inspired by the culinary prowess of Gordon Ramsay, this recipe brings a touch of gourmet flair to your home baking. Perfectly moist, flavorful, and easy to make, it's a delightful treat for any occasion.

Serving: Yields approximately 12 slices.
Preparation Time: 15 minutes
Ready Time: 3 hours (including baking time)

Ingredients:
- 1 cup shredded zucchini, excess moisture squeezed out
- 1 1/2 cups all-purpose flour
- 1/2 teaspoon baking powder
- 1/2 teaspoon baking soda
- 1/4 teaspoon salt
- 2 tablespoons poppy seeds
- Zest of 2 lemons
- 1/2 cup unsalted butter, softened
- 1 cup granulated sugar
- 2 large eggs
- 1 teaspoon vanilla extract
- 1/2 cup plain yogurt
- 1/4 cup fresh lemon juice

Instructions:
1. Preheat your bread machine on the "Quick Bread" setting.

2. In a medium-sized bowl, whisk together the flour, baking powder, baking soda, salt, poppy seeds, and lemon zest. Set aside.
3. In a separate large bowl, cream together the softened butter and sugar until light and fluffy.
4. Add the eggs one at a time, beating well after each addition. Stir in the vanilla extract.
5. Gradually add the dry ingredients to the wet ingredients, alternating with the yogurt, beginning and ending with the dry ingredients.
6. Fold in the shredded zucchini until evenly distributed throughout the batter.
7. Pour in the fresh lemon juice and mix until just combined.
8. Transfer the batter into the bread machine pan, spreading it evenly.
9. Close the lid and select the "Quick Bread" or equivalent setting on your machine. Start the cycle.
10. Once the baking cycle is complete, carefully remove the bread from the machine and allow it to cool on a wire rack before slicing.

Nutrition Information:
(Per serving - 1 slice)
- Calories: 220 kcal
- Total Fat: 10g
- Saturated Fat: 6g
- Trans Fat: 0g
- Cholesterol: 50mg
- Sodium: 180mg
- Total Carbohydrates: 30g
- Dietary Fiber: 1g
- Sugars: 16g
- Protein: 4g

Indulge in the delightful flavors of this Lemon Poppy Seed Zucchini Bread, a testament to the perfect synergy of Gordon Ramsay's inspiration and the convenience of a bread machine. Enjoy it as a breakfast treat, afternoon snack, or dessert—anytime you crave a slice of homemade goodness.

17. Cinnamon Raisin Challah

Indulge your senses in the warm embrace of home-baked goodness with this delightful Cinnamon Raisin Challah, a recipe inspired by the culinary genius of Gordon Ramsay. The rich, sweet aroma of cinnamon and the plump, juicy raisins woven into the soft, golden strands of challah will transport you to a world of comfort and bliss. Perfect for breakfast or as a sweet treat any time of the day, this bread machine recipe ensures a hassle-free baking experience that yields impressive results.

Serving: Makes one large loaf, approximately 12 slices.
Preparation Time: 15 minutes
Ready Time: 3 hours and 30 minutes (includes rising and baking time)

Ingredients:
- 1 cup warm milk
- 1/4 cup unsalted butter, softened
- 2 large eggs
- 1/2 cup granulated sugar
- 1 teaspoon salt
- 4 cups all-purpose flour
- 2 teaspoons active dry yeast
- 1 cup raisins
- 2 teaspoons ground cinnamon

Instructions:
1. Prepare the Bread Machine:
Place the warm milk, softened butter, eggs, granulated sugar, and salt into the bread machine pan.
2. Add Dry Ingredients:
Layer the all-purpose flour on top of the wet ingredients. Make a small well in the center of the flour and add the active dry yeast.
3. Start the Machine:
Set the bread machine to the "Dough" setting and start the cycle. Allow the machine to knead and rise the dough.
4. Incorporate Raisins and Cinnamon:
When the machine signals for add-ins, incorporate the raisins and ground cinnamon. Allow the machine to complete the dough cycle.
5. Shape the Challah:
Once the dough cycle is complete, transfer the dough to a floured surface. Divide it into three equal portions and roll each into a long rope.

Braid the ropes together and place the braided dough on a baking sheet lined with parchment paper.

6. Final Rise:

Cover the braided challah with a clean kitchen towel and let it rise for an additional 30 minutes.

7. Preheat and Bake:

Preheat the oven to 350°F (175°C). Bake the challah for 25-30 minutes or until golden brown.

8. Cool and Enjoy:

Allow the cinnamon raisin challah to cool on a wire rack before slicing. Serve and enjoy the delicious aroma and flavors.

Nutrition Information:
(Per Serving)
- Calories: 220
- Total Fat: 5g
- Saturated Fat: 3g
- Cholesterol: 40mg
- Sodium: 180mg
- Total Carbohydrates: 38g
- Dietary Fiber: 1g
- Sugars: 11g
- Protein: 5g

Note: Nutrition information is approximate and may vary based on specific ingredients used.

18. Smoked Gouda and Bacon Bread

Elevate your bread machine experience with this delectable Smoked Gouda and Bacon Bread, a recipe inspired by the culinary genius of Gordon Ramsay. The rich and smoky flavors of Gouda cheese perfectly complement the savory notes of crispy bacon, resulting in a bread that's not only easy to make but also incredibly indulgent.

Serving: This recipe yields one delicious loaf of Smoked Gouda and Bacon Bread, approximately 12 slices.
Preparation Time: 15 minutes
Ready Time: 3 hours (including rise and bake time)

Ingredients:
- 1 cup warm water (110°F/43°C)
- 2 tablespoons olive oil
- 1 teaspoon sugar
- 1 1/2 teaspoons salt
- 3 cups bread flour
- 2 teaspoons active dry yeast
- 1 cup shredded smoked Gouda cheese
- 1/2 cup cooked and crumbled bacon (about 6 slices)
- Additional olive oil for brushing (optional)

Instructions:
1. In the bread machine pan, combine warm water, olive oil, sugar, and salt.
2. Add the bread flour to the pan, creating a well in the center. Place the active dry yeast in the well.
3. Set the bread machine to the "Basic" or "White Bread" setting, depending on your machine's options. Start the machine.
4. When the machine signals for add-ins (usually during the kneading cycle), add the shredded smoked Gouda cheese and crumbled bacon. Allow the machine to complete the cycle.
5. Once the baking cycle is complete, carefully remove the bread from the machine and let it cool on a wire rack.
6. Optionally, brush the top of the bread with a little olive oil for a shiny finish.
7. Allow the bread to cool for at least 30 minutes before slicing.

Nutrition Information:
Note: Nutrition values are approximate and may vary based on specific ingredients used.
- Serving Size: 1 slice
- Calories: 180
- Total Fat: 7g
- Saturated Fat: 3g
- Trans Fat: 0g
- Cholesterol: 15mg
- Sodium: 350mg
- Total Carbohydrates: 23g
- Dietary Fiber: 1g

- Sugars: 1g
- Protein: 7g

Indulge in the heavenly combination of smoky Gouda and crispy bacon with this bread machine recipe, bringing Gordon Ramsay's culinary inspiration to your home kitchen. Perfect for breakfast, brunch, or as a side to your favorite dishes. Enjoy!

19. Pistachio and Orange Blossom Bread

Elevate your bread machine experience with this delectable Pistachio and Orange Blossom Bread, inspired by the culinary genius Gordon Ramsay. The combination of crunchy pistachios and the delicate essence of orange blossom creates a bread that's not only aromatic but also incredibly flavorful. Perfect for breakfast or as a delightful accompaniment to any meal, this bread is a testament to the artistry of baking.

Serving: Makes one standard-sized loaf
Preparation Time: 15 minutes
Ready Time: 3 hours

Ingredients:
- 1 cup warm water (110°F/43°C)
- 2 tablespoons olive oil
- 3 cups bread flour
- 1/4 cup granulated sugar
- 1 teaspoon salt
- 1 tablespoon active dry yeast
- 1/2 cup shelled pistachios, roughly chopped
- Zest of 1 orange
- 1 teaspoon orange blossom water

Instructions:
1. Place the warm water, olive oil, bread flour, sugar, salt, and active dry yeast in the bread machine pan in the order recommended by the manufacturer.

2. Select the dough setting on your bread machine and press start. Allow the machine to mix and knead the ingredients, letting the dough rise until it has doubled in size.
3. Once the dough cycle is complete, transfer the risen dough to a lightly floured surface. Punch it down and knead in the chopped pistachios, orange zest, and orange blossom water until well distributed.
4. Shape the dough into a loaf and place it into a greased standard-sized bread pan.
5. Cover the pan with a clean kitchen towel and let the dough rise in a warm place for about 1 hour, or until it has doubled in size.
6. Preheat your oven to 375°F (190°C).
7. Bake the bread in the preheated oven for 25-30 minutes or until the top is golden brown and the bread sounds hollow when tapped.
8. Allow the bread to cool in the pan for 10 minutes before transferring it to a wire rack to cool completely.

Nutrition Information:
Note: Nutritional values are approximate and may vary based on specific ingredients used.
- Calories: 180 per slice (based on 12 slices per loaf)
- Total Fat: 5g
- Saturated Fat: 1g
- Trans Fat: 0g
- Cholesterol: 0mg
- Sodium: 200mg
- Total Carbohydrates: 30g
- Dietary Fiber: 2g
- Sugars: 4g
- Protein: 5g

Enjoy the delightful combination of pistachios and orange blossom in every bite of this artisanal bread, inspired by the culinary prowess of Gordon Ramsay. Perfect for any occasion, this bread will surely become a favorite in your home.

20. Basil Pesto Parmesan Knots

Elevate your bread machine creations with the vibrant flavors of Basil Pesto Parmesan Knots. Inspired by the culinary genius of Gordon

Ramsay, these knots are a delightful blend of fragrant basil, rich Parmesan, and the comforting warmth of freshly baked bread. Perfect for a family dinner, a cozy gathering, or as an impressive side for your next dinner party, these knots are sure to be a crowd-pleaser.

Serving: Makes 12 knots
Preparation Time: 15 minutes
Ready Time: 2 hours (including rising time)

Ingredients:
- 1 cup warm water (110°F/43°C)
- 1 tablespoon sugar
- 2 1/4 teaspoons active dry yeast
- 3 cups all-purpose flour
- 1 teaspoon salt
- 1/4 cup olive oil
- 1/2 cup basil pesto
- 1 cup grated Parmesan cheese
- 1/4 cup unsalted butter, melted
- 2 tablespoons chopped fresh basil (for garnish)

Instructions:
1. In the bread machine pan, combine warm water and sugar. Stir until the sugar dissolves. Sprinkle the yeast over the water and let it sit for 5 minutes or until foamy.
2. Add the flour, salt, and olive oil to the bread machine pan. Select the dough setting and start the machine. Allow it to knead and rise until the cycle is complete.
3. Preheat the oven to 375°F (190°C). Line a baking sheet with parchment paper.
4. Once the dough is ready, roll it out on a floured surface into a rectangle, approximately 12x18 inches.
5. Spread the basil pesto evenly over the dough, leaving a small border around the edges. Sprinkle the grated Parmesan cheese over the pesto.
6. Starting from the long edge, roll the dough into a log. Cut the log into 12 equal pieces.
7. Tie each piece into a knot and place them on the prepared baking sheet.
8. Brush the knots with melted butter and bake for 15-20 minutes or until golden brown.

9. Remove from the oven and let the knots cool for a few minutes. Garnish with chopped fresh basil.

Nutrition Information:
(Per serving - 1 knot)
- Calories: 230
- Total Fat: 12g
- Saturated Fat: 4.5g
- Trans Fat: 0g
- Cholesterol: 15mg
- Sodium: 320mg
- Total Carbohydrates: 24g
- Dietary Fiber: 1g
- Sugars: 1g
- Protein: 6g

Note: Nutrition information is approximate and may vary based on specific ingredients and portion sizes.

21. Roasted Red Pepper and Asiago Bread

Elevate your bread machine game with this delectable Roasted Red Pepper and Asiago Bread, inspired by the culinary genius Gordon Ramsay. Bursting with the rich flavors of roasted red peppers and the nutty goodness of Asiago cheese, this bread is a perfect blend of sophistication and comfort. The aroma of this bread baking will fill your kitchen with anticipation, and the taste will leave you craving more.

Serving: Makes one loaf (approximately 12 slices)
Preparation Time: 15 minutes
Ready Time: 3 hours (including rising and baking time)

Ingredients:
- 1 cup roasted red peppers, diced
- 1 cup Asiago cheese, grated
- 3 cups bread flour
- 1 1/2 teaspoons salt
- 1 tablespoon sugar
- 1 cup warm water (110°F/43°C)

- 2 tablespoons olive oil
- 2 1/4 teaspoons active dry yeast

Instructions:
1. In the bread machine pan, add the warm water and sprinkle the yeast over it. Let it sit for 5 minutes until the yeast is dissolved and starts to foam.
2. Add the bread flour, salt, sugar, and olive oil to the yeast mixture in the bread machine pan.
3. Select the "Dough" or "Basic" setting on your bread machine and press start. Allow the machine to mix the ingredients and knead the dough.
4. Once the dough has completed its cycle, remove it from the bread machine and place it on a floured surface.
5. Gently flatten the dough and spread the diced roasted red peppers and grated Asiago cheese evenly over the surface.
6. Roll the dough into a log and place it in a greased loaf pan. Cover it with a clean kitchen towel and let it rise in a warm place for about 1-1.5 hours or until doubled in size.
7. Preheat your oven to 375°F (190°C).
8. Bake the bread in the preheated oven for 25-30 minutes or until the top is golden brown and the bread sounds hollow when tapped.
9. Allow the bread to cool in the pan for 10 minutes before transferring it to a wire rack to cool completely.

Nutrition Information:
Note: Nutritional values are approximate and may vary based on specific ingredients used and portion sizes.
- Calories per serving: 180
- Total Fat: 6g
- Saturated Fat: 2.5g
- Trans Fat: 0g
- Cholesterol: 10mg
- Sodium: 400mg
- Total Carbohydrates: 25g
- Dietary Fiber: 1g
- Sugars: 1g
- Protein: 7g

Enjoy this Roasted Red Pepper and Asiago Bread as a delightful accompaniment to your meals or on its own, and savor the artisanal touch inspired by the renowned Gordon Ramsay.

22. Maple Bacon Bourbon Bread

Indulge your taste buds with a delightful twist on classic bread, inspired by the culinary genius of Gordon Ramsay. Our Maple Bacon Bourbon Bread is a unique creation that combines the rich flavors of maple, the smokiness of bacon, and a hint of bourbon to elevate your bread machine experience. The sweet and savory notes dance harmoniously, creating a loaf that's perfect for any occasion.

Serving: This recipe yields one standard-sized loaf, approximately 12 slices.
Preparation Time: 15 minutes
Ready Time: 3 hours and 30 minutes (including rising and baking time)

Ingredients:
- 1 cup warm water (110°F/43°C)
- 3 tablespoons bourbon
- 1/4 cup pure maple syrup
- 1 teaspoon salt
- 2 tablespoons unsalted butter, softened
- 4 cups bread flour
- 2 teaspoons active dry yeast
- 1/2 cup cooked and crumbled bacon
- 2 tablespoons maple sugar (optional, for sprinkling on top)

Instructions:
1. In the bread machine pan, combine warm water, bourbon, maple syrup, salt, and softened butter.
2. Add the bread flour on top, creating a well in the center. Place the active dry yeast in the well.
3. Insert the bread machine pan into the machine and select the "sweet bread" or "basic" cycle with a light crust setting. Start the machine.
4. Once the machine begins to knead, incorporate the crumbled bacon into the dough.
5. Allow the bread machine to complete the full cycle, including the rising and baking phases.

6. Once the baking is complete, carefully remove the bread pan from the machine and transfer the loaf to a wire rack to cool.
7. If desired, sprinkle the top of the loaf with maple sugar for an extra touch of sweetness.
8. Allow the bread to cool for at least 30 minutes before slicing.

Nutrition Information:
Note: Nutritional values are approximate and may vary based on specific ingredients used.
- Serving Size: 1 slice (1/12 of the loaf)
- Calories: 220
- Total Fat: 5g
- Saturated Fat: 2g
- Trans Fat: 0g
- Cholesterol: 10mg
- Sodium: 230mg
- Total Carbohydrates: 35g
- Dietary Fiber: 1g
- Sugars: 6g
- Protein: 7g

Enjoy this Maple Bacon Bourbon Bread warm with a pat of butter or as a unique addition to your favorite sandwich. Elevate your bread machine game with this Gordon Ramsay-inspired creation that's sure to impress your taste buds and those of your lucky guests!

23. Hazelnut Chocolate Swirl Bread

Indulge your senses with the exquisite blend of rich hazelnuts and decadent chocolate in this Hazelnut Chocolate Swirl Bread. Inspired by the culinary prowess of Gordon Ramsay, this recipe brings a touch of sophistication to your bread machine repertoire. The aroma of freshly baked bread, combined with the irresistible swirls of chocolate and hazelnut, will make this a favorite among friends and family.

Serving: This Hazelnut Chocolate Swirl Bread serves 10-12 slices.
Preparation Time: 15 minutes
Ready Time: 3 hours (including rise and bake time)

Ingredients:
- 1 cup warm milk (110°F/43°C)
- 1/4 cup unsalted butter, softened
- 1/3 cup granulated sugar
- 1 teaspoon salt
- 3 cups all-purpose flour
- 2 1/4 teaspoons active dry yeast
- 1/2 cup hazelnuts, finely chopped
- 1/2 cup chocolate chips or chunks
- 1/4 cup cocoa powder
- 1/4 cup brown sugar
- 1/4 cup unsalted butter, melted

Instructions:
1. In the bread machine pan, combine the warm milk, softened butter, sugar, and salt.
2. Add the flour to the pan, creating a layer on top of the wet ingredients. Make a small well in the center of the flour and add the yeast.
3. Select the dough setting on your bread machine and start the cycle.
4. While the dough is being prepared, mix together the hazelnuts, chocolate chips, cocoa powder, and brown sugar in a small bowl. Set aside.
5. Once the dough cycle is complete, transfer the dough to a floured surface and roll it out into a rectangle.
6. Brush the melted butter over the entire surface of the dough.
7. Evenly sprinkle the hazelnut-chocolate mixture over the buttered dough.
8. Starting from one of the longer sides, tightly roll the dough into a log.
9. Place the rolled dough into a greased loaf pan, cover with a clean kitchen towel, and let it rise in a warm place for about 1 hour or until it doubles in size.
10. Preheat your oven to 350°F (175°C).
11. Bake the bread for 25-30 minutes or until the top is golden brown and the bread sounds hollow when tapped.
12. Allow the Hazelnut Chocolate Swirl Bread to cool in the pan for 10 minutes, then transfer it to a wire rack to cool completely.

Nutrition Information (per serving, based on 12 servings):
- Calories: 290
- Total Fat: 13g

- Saturated Fat: 6g
- Trans Fat: 0g
- Cholesterol: 20mg
- Sodium: 220mg
- Total Carbohydrates: 38g
- Dietary Fiber: 2g
- Sugars: 11g
- Protein: 5g

Enjoy this Hazelnut Chocolate Swirl Bread as a delightful treat for breakfast or a sweet indulgence during afternoon tea. The harmonious blend of flavors will surely make it a standout in your collection of bread machine recipes.

24. Prosciutto and Rosemary Fougasse

Elevate your bread machine repertoire with the exquisite Prosciutto and Rosemary Fougasse inspired by the culinary genius of Gordon Ramsay. This bread, with its delicate folds of prosciutto and aromatic rosemary, is a testament to the artistry of combining simple ingredients to create a masterpiece. Perfect for sharing or savoring alone, this fougasse brings the flavors of the Mediterranean right to your table.

Serving: Makes 1 Fougasse (8 servings)
Preparation Time: 15 minutes
Ready Time: 3 hours (including rising and baking time)

Ingredients:
- 1 cup warm water (110°F/43°C)
- 2 tablespoons olive oil
- 1 teaspoon honey
- 3 cups bread flour
- 1 ½ teaspoons salt
- 2 teaspoons active dry yeast
- 4 slices prosciutto, torn into pieces
- 2 tablespoons fresh rosemary, finely chopped
- Extra olive oil for brushing

Instructions:

1. In the bread machine pan, combine warm water, olive oil, and honey.
2. Add the bread flour on top, creating a well in the center. Place salt in one corner and yeast in another, ensuring they do not come into direct contact.
3. Insert the bread machine pan into the machine and select the dough setting. Start the machine.
4. Once the dough is ready, preheat your oven to 400°F (200°C). Line a baking sheet with parchment paper.
5. Turn the dough out onto a floured surface and gently shape it into an oval. With a sharp knife, make diagonal cuts on both sides of the oval, leaving a thicker portion in the center.
6. Gently pull apart the dough along the cuts, creating a leaf-like shape. Stretch it slightly to accentuate the openings.
7. Place torn prosciutto pieces and chopped rosemary into the openings. Press them gently into the dough.
8. Transfer the shaped fougasse onto the prepared baking sheet. Brush the top with olive oil.
9. Bake for 20-25 minutes or until golden brown and crisp. Cool on a wire rack.

Nutrition Information (per serving):
- Calories: 180
- Total Fat: 5g
- Saturated Fat: 1g
- Trans Fat: 0g
- Cholesterol: 5mg
- Sodium: 380mg
- Total Carbohydrates: 29g
- Dietary Fiber: 2g
- Sugars: 1g
- Protein: 5g

Indulge in the irresistible flavors of this Prosciutto and Rosemary Fougasse – a bread machine creation that effortlessly combines simplicity and sophistication. Enjoy it fresh out of the oven, and let the aroma of rosemary and prosciutto transport you to the heart of Mediterranean cuisine.

25. Everything Bagel Bread

Elevate your bread machine game with this delightful Everything Bagel Bread inspired by the culinary genius of Gordon Ramsay. Imagine the classic flavors of an everything bagel seamlessly woven into a soft and fluffy loaf. This recipe is a testament to the fusion of convenience and gourmet taste, making it a must-try for bread enthusiasts and novices alike. Enjoy the aromatic blend of sesame seeds, poppy seeds, garlic, onion, and more in every delicious slice.

Serving: 12 slices
Preparation Time: 15 minutes
Ready Time: 3 hours and 30 minutes (including rise and bake time)

Ingredients:
- 1 cup warm water (110°F/43°C)
- 2 tablespoons olive oil
- 3 cups bread flour
- 2 tablespoons sugar
- 1 teaspoon salt
- 1 1/2 teaspoons active dry yeast

For the Everything Bagel Topping:
- 1 tablespoon sesame seeds
- 1 tablespoon poppy seeds
- 1 tablespoon dried minced garlic
- 1 tablespoon dried minced onion
- 1 teaspoon coarse salt

Instructions:
1. Prepare the Bread Dough:
- In the bread machine pan, combine warm water and olive oil.
- Add bread flour, sugar, salt, and active dry yeast in layers, following the manufacturer's instructions for your specific bread machine.
- Select the dough setting and start the machine.
2. Rise:
- Once the dough cycle is complete, transfer the dough to a lightly floured surface.
- Knead the dough a few times, shaping it into a smooth ball.

- Place the dough in a greased bowl, cover with a clean kitchen towel, and let it rise in a warm place for about 1-2 hours or until doubled in size.

3. Shape the Loaf:
- Punch down the risen dough and turn it out onto a floured surface.
- Roll the dough into a rectangle and then roll it up tightly, starting from the short side.
- Place the rolled dough seam side down in a greased 9x5-inch loaf pan.

4. Everything Bagel Topping:
- In a small bowl, combine sesame seeds, poppy seeds, dried minced garlic, dried minced onion, and coarse salt.
- Brush the top of the dough with water and sprinkle the everything bagel topping evenly over the surface.

5. Second Rise:
- Cover the loaf pan with a kitchen towel and let the dough rise for an additional 30-60 minutes, or until it reaches the top of the pan.

6. Bake:
- Preheat your oven to 375°F (190°C).
- Bake the bread for 25-30 minutes or until golden brown.
- Allow the bread to cool in the pan for 10 minutes, then transfer it to a wire rack to cool completely.

7. Slice and Enjoy:
- Once cooled, slice the Everything Bagel Bread into 12 delicious slices.

Nutrition Information:
(per slice)
- Calories: 150
- Total Fat: 4g
- Saturated Fat: 0.5g
- Cholesterol: 0mg
- Sodium: 300mg
- Total Carbohydrates: 25g
- Dietary Fiber: 2g
- Sugars: 1g
- Protein: 4g

Indulge in the delightful flavors of this Everything Bagel Bread – a perfect blend of simplicity and sophistication that will leave your taste buds craving more. Enjoy it toasted with cream cheese or as the perfect complement to your favorite sandwiches.

26. Blueberry Lemon Almond Loaf

Indulge your taste buds in a delightful symphony of flavors with our Blueberry Lemon Almond Loaf, a creation inspired by the culinary genius of Gordon Ramsay. This bread machine recipe brings together the tartness of fresh blueberries, the zesty brightness of lemons, and the nutty richness of almonds, resulting in a loaf that's both moist and bursting with flavor.

Serving: Makes one delicious Blueberry Lemon Almond Loaf.
Preparation Time: 15 minutes
Ready Time: 3 hours

Ingredients:
- 1 cup fresh blueberries
- 1 tablespoon lemon zest
- 1/4 cup fresh lemon juice
- 1/2 cup unsalted butter, softened
- 3/4 cup granulated sugar
- 2 large eggs
- 1 teaspoon vanilla extract
- 2 cups all-purpose flour
- 1/2 cup almond flour
- 1 1/2 teaspoons baking powder
- 1/2 teaspoon baking soda
- 1/2 teaspoon salt
- 1 cup buttermilk

Instructions:
1. Preheat your bread machine on the "Quick Bread" or "Cake" setting.
2. In a medium bowl, toss the fresh blueberries with 1 tablespoon of all-purpose flour. This helps prevent the blueberries from sinking to the bottom of the loaf during baking.
3. In a large mixing bowl, cream together the softened butter and granulated sugar until light and fluffy.
4. Add the eggs one at a time, beating well after each addition. Stir in the vanilla extract, lemon zest, and lemon juice.

5. In a separate bowl, whisk together the all-purpose flour, almond flour, baking powder, baking soda, and salt.
6. Gradually add the dry ingredients to the wet ingredients, alternating with the buttermilk. Begin and end with the dry ingredients. Mix until just combined.
7. Gently fold in the flour-coated blueberries, ensuring even distribution throughout the batter.
8. Pour the batter into the bread machine pan and smooth the top with a spatula.
9. Close the lid and select the "Quick Bread" or "Cake" setting. Start the machine.
10. Once the baking cycle is complete, carefully remove the loaf from the bread machine and let it cool in the pan for 10 minutes. Then transfer the loaf to a wire rack to cool completely.

Nutrition Information:
(Per serving, assuming 12 slices)
- Calories: 250
- Total Fat: 11g
- Saturated Fat: 6g
- Cholesterol: 50mg
- Sodium: 220mg
- Total Carbohydrates: 32g
- Dietary Fiber: 2g
- Sugars: 15g
- Protein: 4g

Indulge in this exquisite Blueberry Lemon Almond Loaf, a testament to the perfect marriage of sweet and tangy flavors. Inspired by the culinary mastery of Gordon Ramsay, this bread machine recipe is sure to become a staple in your home.

27. Irish Soda Bread with Golden Raisins

Elevate your bread machine game with this delightful recipe inspired by Gordon Ramsay—Irish Soda Bread with Golden Raisins. The rustic charm of traditional Irish soda bread meets the subtle sweetness of golden raisins, creating a loaf that's both comforting and sophisticated. Easy to make in your trusty bread machine, this recipe promises a taste of Ireland's rich culinary heritage with a touch of Ramsay's culinary finesse.

Serving: Makes one hearty loaf, perfect for sharing with friends and family.
Preparation Time: 15 minutes
Ready Time: 2 hours and 30 minutes

Ingredients:
- 3 cups all-purpose flour
- 1 cup whole wheat flour
- 1 teaspoon baking soda
- 1 teaspoon salt
- 1 and 3/4 cups buttermilk
- 1/4 cup honey
- 1 cup golden raisins
- Butter (for serving, optional)

Instructions:
1. Place the ingredients in your bread machine in the following order: buttermilk, honey, all-purpose flour, whole wheat flour, baking soda, and salt. Ensure the dry ingredients are on top, forming a well in the center.
2. Set your bread machine to the "Basic" or "White Bread" setting with a medium crust. Start the machine.
3. When the machine signals for additions or after the first kneading cycle, add the golden raisins. This ensures they are evenly distributed throughout the dough.
4. Once the cycle is complete, transfer the dough to a floured surface. Knead it lightly, incorporating additional flour if necessary, until it forms a smooth ball.
5. Preheat your oven to 375°F (190°C).
6. Place the dough on a parchment-lined baking sheet. Using a sharp knife, make a deep "X" across the top of the loaf.
7. Bake for 40-45 minutes or until the bread is golden brown and sounds hollow when tapped on the bottom.
8. Allow the bread to cool on a wire rack before slicing. Serve with butter, if desired.

Nutrition Information:

Note: Nutrition values are approximate and may vary based on specific ingredients used.
- Serving Size: 1 slice (1/12 of the loaf)
- Calories: 220
- Total Fat: 1.5g
- Saturated Fat: 0.5g
- Cholesterol: 2mg
- Sodium: 330mg
- Total Carbohydrates: 46g
- Dietary Fiber: 2g
- Sugars: 13g
- Protein: 5g

Enjoy the delightful combination of Irish tradition and Gordon Ramsay's culinary flair in every slice of this Golden Raisin Irish Soda Bread!

28. Spinach and Feta Pull-Apart Bread

Elevate your bread machine game with this delightful Spinach and Feta Pull-Apart Bread inspired by the culinary genius of Gordon Ramsay. The combination of earthy spinach and tangy feta cheese creates a savory explosion in every bite. Perfect for sharing with loved ones or as a standout appetizer at your next gathering, this recipe is a testament to the fusion of simplicity and sophistication.

Serving: Makes 1 pull-apart bread loaf, approximately 10 servings.
Preparation Time: 15 minutes
Ready Time: 3 hours (including dough rising time)

Ingredients:
- 1 cup fresh spinach, chopped
- 1 cup feta cheese, crumbled
- 3 cups all-purpose flour
- 1 1/2 teaspoons salt
- 1 tablespoon sugar
- 1 cup warm water
- 2 tablespoons olive oil
- 1 packet (2 1/4 teaspoons) active dry yeast
- 1/2 teaspoon garlic powder

- 1/2 teaspoon dried oregano
- 1/4 teaspoon black pepper
- Olive oil or melted butter for brushing

Instructions:
1. Prepare the Dough:
- In the bread machine pan, combine warm water, sugar, and active dry yeast. Allow it to sit for 5 minutes until the yeast activates and becomes foamy.
- Add the flour, salt, and olive oil to the pan. Select the dough cycle and start the machine. Let it knead and rise the dough.
2. Prepare the Filling:
- In a bowl, mix chopped spinach, crumbled feta, garlic powder, dried oregano, and black pepper. Set aside.
3. Assemble the Bread:
- Once the dough cycle is complete, transfer the dough to a floured surface. Roll it out into a rectangle (approximately 12x18 inches).
- Spread the spinach and feta mixture evenly over the dough.
4. Shape the Bread:
- Cut the dough into strips, then stack the strips on top of each other. Cut the stack into squares.
- Carefully place the squares into a greased loaf pan, allowing layers to separate slightly.
5. Second Rise:
- Cover the pan with a clean kitchen towel and let it rise for an additional 30-45 minutes or until doubled in size.
6. Bake:
- Preheat the oven to 350°F (175°C).
- Bake the bread for 25-30 minutes or until golden brown.
7. Finish and Serve:
- Brush the top of the bread with olive oil or melted butter.
- Allow the bread to cool for a few minutes before serving. Pull apart the layers for a visually stunning and shareable bread experience.

Nutrition Information:
(Per Serving)
- Calories: 220
- Total Fat: 8g
- Saturated Fat: 4g
- Cholesterol: 20mg

- Sodium: 420mg
- Total Carbohydrates: 30g
- Dietary Fiber: 2g
- Sugars: 1g
- Protein: 8g

Indulge in the rich flavors of this Spinach and Feta Pull-Apart Bread, a delightful creation that blends the expertise of Gordon Ramsay with the convenience of your trusty bread machine.

29. Buttermilk Honey Wheat Bread

Indulge your taste buds in the wholesome goodness of Buttermilk Honey Wheat Bread—a delectable creation inspired by the culinary genius, Gordon Ramsay. This bread machine recipe combines the richness of buttermilk, the sweetness of honey, and the heartiness of whole wheat flour to deliver a loaf that's both flavorful and nourishing. Follow along and let your bread machine do the work as you embark on a delightful journey of baking mastery.

Serving: Makes one 2-pound loaf (approximately 16 slices).
Preparation Time: 15 minutes
Ready Time: 3 hours 30 minutes (includes rising and baking time)

Ingredients:
- 1 cup buttermilk, room temperature
- 1/4 cup honey
- 2 tablespoons unsalted butter, softened
- 3 cups whole wheat flour
- 1 cup all-purpose flour
- 1 1/2 teaspoons salt
- 1 1/2 teaspoons active dry yeast

Instructions:
1. Place the ingredients into your bread machine in the order recommended by the manufacturer.
2. Select the whole wheat or whole grain setting on your bread machine. If your machine allows you to choose the crust color, select your preference.

3. Start the machine and let it work its magic. Be sure to monitor the dough during the first few minutes of mixing to ensure proper consistency. Adjust with additional flour or liquid if needed.
4. Once the baking cycle is complete, carefully remove the hot bread from the machine and transfer it to a wire rack to cool.
5. Allow the bread to cool for at least 30 minutes before slicing. This will help the loaf set and make for easier cutting.
6. Slice and serve this Buttermilk Honey Wheat Bread on its own, with a pat of butter, or alongside your favorite spreads and cheeses.

Nutrition Information:
Per Serving (1 slice):
- Calories: 130
- Total Fat: 2g
- Saturated Fat: 1g
- Trans Fat: 0g
- Cholesterol: 5mg
- Sodium: 180mg
- Total Carbohydrates: 25g
- Dietary Fiber: 3g
- Sugars: 5g
- Protein: 4g

Note: Nutritional values are approximate and may vary based on specific ingredients and portion sizes.

30. Roquefort and Walnut Batard

Indulge your taste buds in the delightful harmony of flavors with our Roquefort and Walnut Batard, a masterpiece inspired by the culinary genius of Gordon Ramsay. This bread machine recipe brings together the rich, tangy notes of Roquefort cheese and the earthy crunch of walnuts, creating a bread that's not just a side dish but a star on its own. Elevate your baking game with this sophisticated and delicious bread that's sure to impress both family and friends.

Serving: Makes 1 Roquefort and Walnut Batard, approximately 12 slices.
Preparation Time: 15 minutes
Ready Time: 3 hours 30 minutes

Ingredients:
- 1 cup warm water (about 110°F/43°C)
- 2 tablespoons olive oil
- 1 teaspoon honey
- 1 teaspoon salt
- 3 cups bread flour
- 2 teaspoons active dry yeast
- 1/2 cup crumbled Roquefort cheese
- 1/2 cup chopped walnuts

Instructions:
1. Prepare the Bread Machine:
- Ensure your bread machine is clean and in good working condition.
- Insert the kneading paddle into the machine pan.
2. Combine Wet Ingredients:
- In a bowl, mix warm water, olive oil, and honey until well combined.
3. Add Dry Ingredients to Bread Machine:
- In the bread machine pan, layer the flour, salt, and active dry yeast.
- Pour the wet ingredients over the dry ingredients in the machine pan.
4. Knead the Dough:
- Place the machine pan into the bread machine and select the dough or manual cycle.
- Allow the machine to knead the dough until it forms a smooth, elastic ball.
5. Incorporate Roquefort and Walnuts:
- About 5 minutes before the kneading cycle is complete, add the crumbled Roquefort cheese and chopped walnuts to the dough. Let the machine incorporate them evenly.
6. Let the Dough Rise:
- Once the dough cycle is complete, transfer the dough to a lightly floured surface.
- Shape it into a batard (oval loaf) and place it on a parchment-lined baking sheet.
- Cover with a clean kitchen towel and let it rise for about 1 to 1.5 hours or until doubled in size.
7. Preheat and Bake:
- Preheat your oven to 375°F (190°C) during the last 15 minutes of the rising time.

- Bake the Roquefort and Walnut Batard for 25-30 minutes or until golden brown.
8. Cool and Serve:
- Allow the bread to cool on a wire rack before slicing.
- Serve and enjoy the delightful combination of Roquefort and walnuts in every bite.

Nutrition Information (per serving - 1 slice):
- Calories: 180
- Total Fat: 8g
- Saturated Fat: 2g
- Trans Fat: 0g
- Cholesterol: 5mg
- Sodium: 280mg
- Total Carbohydrates: 21g
- Dietary Fiber: 2g
- Sugars: 1g
- Protein: 6g

Note: Nutrition information is approximate and may vary based on specific ingredients and serving sizes.

31. Cranberry Orange Cinnamon Swirl Bread

Elevate your bread machine experience with this delectable Cranberry Orange Cinnamon Swirl Bread inspired by the culinary genius of Gordon Ramsay. Bursting with the vibrant flavors of tart cranberries, zesty orange, and warm cinnamon, this bread is a delightful fusion of sweet and tangy. Perfect for breakfast or a cozy afternoon treat, each slice is a testament to the artistry of bread-making.

Serving: 12 slices
Preparation Time: 15 minutes
Ready Time: 3 hours

Ingredients:
- 1 cup warm milk (about 110°F/43°C)
- 1/4 cup unsalted butter, softened
- 1/4 cup granulated sugar

- Zest of 1 orange
- 1 teaspoon vanilla extract
- 3 cups all-purpose flour
- 1 teaspoon salt
- 1 tablespoon active dry yeast
- 1/2 cup dried cranberries
- 1/3 cup brown sugar
- 1 teaspoon ground cinnamon

Instructions:
1. Place the warm milk, softened butter, granulated sugar, orange zest, vanilla extract, flour, salt, and yeast in the bread machine pan in the order recommended by the manufacturer.
2. Select the dough setting on your bread machine and start the cycle. Allow the machine to knead and rise the dough, typically taking about 1.5 to 2 hours.
3. While the dough is rising, mix together the dried cranberries, brown sugar, and ground cinnamon in a small bowl. Set aside.
4. Once the dough cycle is complete, transfer the dough to a floured surface. Roll it out into a rectangle, approximately 12 x 18 inches.
5. Sprinkle the cranberry-cinnamon sugar mixture evenly over the rolled-out dough.
6. Starting from one of the longer edges, tightly roll the dough into a log. Pinch the seam to seal.
7. Place the rolled dough into a greased 9x5-inch loaf pan, seam side down.
8. Cover the pan with a clean kitchen towel and let the dough rise in a warm place for about 1 hour or until it has doubled in size.
9. Preheat the oven to 350°F (180°C).
10. Bake the bread for 25-30 minutes or until it is golden brown and sounds hollow when tapped on the bottom.
11. Allow the bread to cool in the pan for 10 minutes before transferring it to a wire rack to cool completely.

Nutrition Information (per slice):
- Calories: 210
- Total Fat: 5g
- Saturated Fat: 3g
- Cholesterol: 15mg
- Sodium: 200mg

- Total Carbohydrates: 37g
- Dietary Fiber: 1g
- Sugars: 12g
- Protein: 4g

Enjoy this Cranberry Orange Cinnamon Swirl Bread with a cup of tea or coffee for a delightful culinary experience inspired by Gordon Ramsay.

32. Ancho Chili Chocolate Sourdough

Indulge your taste buds in a symphony of bold flavors with our Ancho Chili Chocolate Sourdough, a unique creation inspired by the culinary genius of Gordon Ramsay. This bread machine recipe combines the rich warmth of ancho chili with the decadent allure of chocolate, resulting in a loaf that's both spicy and sweet, perfect for those who crave an adventurous twist to their daily bread.

Serving: Makes one hearty loaf, approximately 12 slices.
Preparation Time: 15 minutes
Ready Time: 4 hours (including rising and baking time)

Ingredients:
- 1 cup active sourdough starter
- 1 1/2 cups bread flour
- 1 cup whole wheat flour
- 1/2 cup dark rye flour
- 2 tablespoons cocoa powder
- 1 tablespoon ancho chili powder
- 1 teaspoon salt
- 1/4 cup honey
- 1/4 cup olive oil
- 3/4 cup warm water
- 1/2 cup dark chocolate chips

Instructions:
1. In the bread machine pan, combine the active sourdough starter, bread flour, whole wheat flour, dark rye flour, cocoa powder, ancho chili powder, and salt.

2. In a separate bowl, mix the honey, olive oil, and warm water. Add this liquid mixture to the bread machine pan.
3. Set the bread machine to the dough setting and start the cycle. Allow the machine to knead and rise the dough.
4. Once the dough cycle is complete, gently fold in the dark chocolate chips, ensuring they are evenly distributed throughout the dough.
5. Remove the dough from the machine and shape it into a round loaf. Place the dough in a greased and floured Dutch oven or on a parchment-lined baking sheet.
6. Cover the dough with a clean kitchen towel and let it rise for an additional 1-2 hours, or until it has doubled in size.
7. Preheat your oven to 375°F (190°C). If using a Dutch oven, bake with the lid on for 20 minutes, then remove the lid and bake for an additional 15-20 minutes, or until the bread is golden brown and sounds hollow when tapped. If using a baking sheet, bake for 25-30 minutes.
8. Allow the Ancho Chili Chocolate Sourdough to cool before slicing.

Nutrition Information:
(Per serving - 1 slice)
- Calories: 180
- Total Fat: 7g
- Saturated Fat: 2g
- Cholesterol: 0mg
- Sodium: 170mg
- Total Carbohydrates: 27g
- Dietary Fiber: 3g
- Sugars: 4g
- Protein: 4g

Note: Nutrition information is approximate and may vary based on specific ingredients used.

33. Pumpkin Sage Dinner Rolls

Indulge your taste buds in the exquisite blend of autumn flavors with these Pumpkin Sage Dinner Rolls, a delightful creation inspired by the culinary genius of Gordon Ramsay. These soft and fragrant rolls are a perfect accompaniment to any meal, adding a touch of warmth and sophistication to your dining experience.

Serving: Makes 12 rolls
Preparation Time: 15 minutes
Ready Time: 2 hours (including rising time)

Ingredients:
- 1 cup canned pumpkin puree
- 1/2 cup warm milk (about 110°F/43°C)
- 1/4 cup unsalted butter, melted
- 1/4 cup honey
- 1 large egg
- 1 teaspoon salt
- 3 1/2 cups all-purpose flour
- 2 1/4 teaspoons active dry yeast
- 2 tablespoons fresh sage, finely chopped

Instructions:
1. Prepare the Bread Machine:
Place the ingredients in the bread machine in the order recommended by the manufacturer.
2. Kneading and Rising:
Set the bread machine to the dough setting and let it run through the kneading and first rising cycle. This usually takes about 1.5 hours.
3. Add Sage:
When the machine signals that it has completed the first rise, add the chopped sage to the dough. Allow the machine to continue until the cycle is complete.
4. Divide and Shape:
Turn the dough out onto a floured surface and divide it into 12 equal portions. Shape each portion into a smooth ball.
5. Second Rise:
Place the shaped rolls in a greased baking pan, cover with a clean kitchen towel, and let them rise for an additional 30-45 minutes, or until they have doubled in size.
6. Preheat and Bake:
Preheat your oven to 375°F (190°C). Bake the rolls for 15-20 minutes or until they are golden brown on top.
7. Brush with Butter:
Remove the rolls from the oven and brush the tops with melted butter for a glossy finish.

8. Cool and Serve:
Allow the Pumpkin Sage Dinner Rolls to cool slightly before serving. Enjoy them warm with your favorite main course or as a standalone treat.

Nutrition Information (per serving):
Calories: 180 | Total Fat: 5g | Saturated Fat: 3g | Cholesterol: 25mg | Sodium: 200mg | Total Carbohydrates: 31g | Dietary Fiber: 2g | Sugars: 7g | Protein: 4g

These Pumpkin Sage Dinner Rolls are a delightful addition to your bread-making repertoire, showcasing the perfect harmony of pumpkin sweetness and earthy sage. Elevate your dining experience with the warmth and aroma of these delectable rolls, sure to impress even the most discerning palates.

34. Apricot Pistachio Challah

Elevate your bread machine game with this exquisite Apricot Pistachio Challah, a delightful creation inspired by the culinary genius of Gordon Ramsay. The fusion of sweet apricots and crunchy pistachios makes this challah a unique and irresistible treat. Perfect for any occasion, this bread machine recipe is not only delicious but also a testament to the artistry of bread-making.

Serving: This Apricot Pistachio Challah yields one beautiful loaf, serving approximately 10 slices.
Preparation Time: 15 minutes
Ready Time: 3 hours (includes rising and baking time)

Ingredients:
- 1 cup warm water
- 3 tablespoons olive oil
- 1/4 cup honey
- 3 large eggs
- 4 cups bread flour
- 1 teaspoon salt
- 2 teaspoons active dry yeast
- 1/2 cup dried apricots, chopped

- 1/2 cup shelled pistachios, chopped

Instructions:
1. Place the warm water, olive oil, honey, and eggs into the bread machine pan.
2. In a separate bowl, whisk together the bread flour and salt.
3. Add the flour mixture to the bread machine pan, creating a layer on top of the wet ingredients.
4. Make a small well in the center of the flour and add the yeast.
5. Set the bread machine to the dough setting and start the cycle. Allow it to mix and knead the dough thoroughly.
6. Once the dough has completed its cycle, transfer it to a lightly floured surface.
7. Gently flatten the dough and sprinkle chopped apricots and pistachios evenly over the surface.
8. Roll the dough into a log, ensuring the apricots and pistachios are distributed evenly.
9. Place the rolled dough into a greased loaf pan, cover with a kitchen towel, and let it rise in a warm place for about 1 hour or until doubled in size.
10. Preheat your oven to 350°F (175°C).
11. Bake the challah for 25-30 minutes or until it achieves a golden-brown color.
12. Allow the bread to cool in the pan for 10 minutes, then transfer it to a wire rack to cool completely.

Nutrition Information (per serving):
- Calories: 250
- Total Fat: 8g
- Saturated Fat: 1.5g
- Trans Fat: 0g
- Cholesterol: 50mg
- Sodium: 220mg
- Total Carbohydrates: 38g
- Dietary Fiber: 2g
- Sugars: 8g
- Protein: 7g

Note: Nutrition information is approximate and may vary based on specific ingredients and serving sizes.

35. Asiago and Black Pepper Baguette

Indulge in the exquisite flavors of a culinary masterpiece with our Asiago and Black Pepper Baguette. Inspired by the culinary genius of Gordon Ramsay, this bread machine recipe combines the rich and nutty notes of Asiago cheese with the bold kick of black pepper, resulting in a baguette that's both sophisticated and comforting. Elevate your bread-making skills to new heights and treat your senses to a delightful symphony of flavors.

Serving: Yields one hearty Asiago and Black Pepper Baguette.
Preparation Time: 15 minutes
Ready Time: 3 hours (including rise and bake time)

Ingredients:
- 1 cup warm water (110°F/43°C)
- 2 tablespoons olive oil
- 3 cups bread flour
- 1 teaspoon sugar
- 1 ½ teaspoons salt
- 1 teaspoon freshly ground black pepper
- 1 cup shredded Asiago cheese
- 2 ¼ teaspoons active dry yeast

Instructions:
1. Place the warm water and olive oil into the bread machine pan.
2. In a separate bowl, whisk together the bread flour, sugar, salt, and black pepper.
3. Add the dry ingredients to the bread machine pan on top of the water and oil.
4. Sprinkle the shredded Asiago cheese over the dry ingredients.
5. Make a well in the center of the dry ingredients and add the active dry yeast.
6. Place the bread machine pan into the bread machine, secure the pan in place, and select the "Dough" cycle.
7. Once the cycle is complete, remove the dough from the machine and place it on a lightly floured surface.
8. Preheat the oven to 375°F (190°C).

9. Shape the dough into a baguette and place it on a baking sheet.
10. Allow the baguette to rise for an additional 30 minutes.
11. Bake in the preheated oven for 25-30 minutes or until golden brown.
12. Let the Asiago and Black Pepper Baguette cool before slicing.

Nutrition Information:
(Per Serving)
- Calories: 180
- Total Fat: 6g
- Saturated Fat: 2g
- Trans Fat: 0g
- Cholesterol: 10mg
- Sodium: 280mg
- Total Carbohydrates: 26g
- Dietary Fiber: 1g
- Sugars: 0g
- Protein: 6g

Note: Nutrition information is approximate and may vary based on specific ingredients and portion sizes.

36. Spelt and Honey Boule

Discover the delightful combination of ancient grains and natural sweetness with this Spelt and Honey Boule. Inspired by the culinary genius of Gordon Ramsay, this bread machine recipe brings together the wholesome goodness of spelt flour and the rich flavor of honey. The result is a hearty and flavorful boule that's perfect for any occasion, whether you're enjoying it with a savory spread or savoring it on its own. Let your bread machine do the work, and indulge in the comforting aroma of freshly baked bread.

Serving: Makes one round boule, approximately 10 slices.
Preparation Time: 15 minutes
Ready Time: 3 hours

Ingredients:
- 1 1/2 cups warm water
- 2 tablespoons olive oil

- 1/4 cup honey
- 3 1/2 cups spelt flour
- 1 teaspoon salt
- 2 teaspoons active dry yeast

Instructions:
1. Place the warm water, olive oil, and honey into the bread machine pan.
2. In a separate bowl, combine the spelt flour and salt.
3. Add the flour mixture to the bread machine pan on top of the wet ingredients.
4. Make a small well in the center of the flour and add the active dry yeast.
5. Place the bread machine pan into the bread machine and select the "Dough" setting.
6. Allow the machine to run its cycle, mixing and kneading the dough. This typically takes about 1.5 to 2 hours.
7. Once the dough cycle is complete, transfer the dough to a floured surface and shape it into a round boule.
8. Place the boule on a parchment paper-lined baking sheet and cover it with a clean kitchen towel. Allow it to rise for an additional 30-60 minutes, or until it doubles in size.
9. Preheat the oven to 375°F (190°C).
10. Optionally, slash the top of the boule with a sharp knife to create a decorative pattern.
11. Bake in the preheated oven for 25-30 minutes or until the bread is golden brown and sounds hollow when tapped on the bottom.
12. Allow the Spelt and Honey Boule to cool before slicing and serving.

Nutrition Information (per slice, assuming 10 slices):
- Calories: 180
- Total Fat: 3g
- Saturated Fat: 0.5g
- Cholesterol: 0mg
- Sodium: 230mg
- Total Carbohydrates: 35g
- Dietary Fiber: 5g
- Sugars: 7g
- Protein: 6g

Enjoy the wholesome goodness of this Spelt and Honey Boule, a bread machine creation that elevates your bread game with the unique blend of spelt flour and natural sweetness. Perfect for any meal or snack, this boule is sure to become a staple in your home.

37. Sunflower Seed Rye Bread

Indulge your taste buds in the wholesome goodness of Sunflower Seed Rye Bread—a delectable creation inspired by the culinary genius, Gordon Ramsay. This hearty bread combines the earthy flavors of rye with the nutty richness of sunflower seeds, resulting in a loaf that's not only delicious but also packed with nutritional benefits. Baking this bread using a bread machine ensures a fuss-free process, allowing you to savor the delightful aroma of fresh bread wafting through your kitchen.

Serving: Makes one 2-pound loaf.
Preparation Time: 15 minutes
Ready Time: 3 hours 30 minutes

Ingredients:
- 1 1/2 cups warm water (110°F/43°C)
- 2 tablespoons olive oil
- 2 tablespoons honey
- 1 1/2 teaspoons salt
- 1 cup rye flour
- 2 1/2 cups bread flour
- 1/2 cup sunflower seeds
- 2 teaspoons active dry yeast

Instructions:
1. Prepare the Bread Machine:
Place the warm water, olive oil, honey, and salt in the bread machine pan.
2. Add Dry Ingredients:
Layer the rye flour, bread flour, and sunflower seeds over the wet ingredients.
3. Create a Well for Yeast:
Make a well in the center of the dry ingredients and add the active dry yeast.
4. Select the Setting:

Set your bread machine to the "Whole Wheat" or "Rye Bread" setting, depending on your machine's options.
5. Start the Machine:
Start the bread machine, allowing it to complete the kneading, rising, and baking cycles.
6. Check for Consistency:
After the kneading cycle, check the dough's consistency. If it seems too dry, add a tablespoon of water; if too wet, add a tablespoon of flour.
7. Wait Patiently:
Allow the bread machine to work its magic, and revel in the anticipation of the delightful aroma.
8. Cool and Slice:
Once the baking cycle is complete, carefully remove the bread from the machine and let it cool on a wire rack. Once cooled, slice and enjoy!

Nutrition Information:
* (Per Serving - 1 slice, based on 16 slices per loaf)
- Calories: 150
- Total Fat: 5g
- Saturated Fat: 0.5g
- Cholesterol: 0mg
- Sodium: 180mg
- Total Carbohydrates: 23g
- Dietary Fiber: 3g
- Sugars: 2g
- Protein: 5g
Note: Nutrition information is approximate and may vary based on specific ingredients and serving sizes.

38. Lemon Thyme Focaccia

Lemon Thyme Focaccia is a delightful twist on the classic Italian bread, blending the zesty brightness of lemon with the earthy fragrance of thyme. Inspired by Gordon Ramsay's innovative culinary style, this recipe takes the simplicity of focaccia to new heights, perfecting it for the bread machine. The result is a fragrant, golden loaf with a tantalizing aroma and a burst of fresh flavors in every bite.

Serving: This recipe yields one loaf of Lemon Thyme Focaccia, approximately 12 servings.
Preparation Time: 15 minutes
Ready Time: 3 hours (including rising and baking time)

Ingredients:
- 1 cup warm water
- 2 tablespoons olive oil
- 3 cups bread flour
- 1 1/2 teaspoons instant yeast
- 1 teaspoon salt
- Zest of 1 lemon
- 2 tablespoons fresh thyme leaves
- Additional olive oil for brushing
- Coarse sea salt, for topping

Instructions:
1. Begin by adding the warm water and olive oil to the bread machine's pan.
2. In a separate bowl, mix the bread flour, instant yeast, and salt together.
3. Gradually add the dry mixture to the bread machine's pan.
4. Add the lemon zest and fresh thyme leaves to the pan.
5. Set the bread machine to the dough cycle and start.
6. Once the dough cycle is complete, remove the dough and place it on a lightly floured surface.
7. Preheat the oven to 400°F (200°C).
8. Flatten the dough into a rectangular or round shape, about 1/2 inch thick, on a baking sheet lined with parchment paper.
9. Cover the dough with a clean kitchen towel and let it rise for another 30-40 minutes in a warm place.
10. After rising, use your fingers to make dimples all over the dough's surface.
11. Drizzle the top generously with olive oil and sprinkle coarse sea salt over it.
12. Bake in the preheated oven for 20-25 minutes or until golden brown and cooked through.
13. Once baked, remove from the oven and let it cool on a wire rack before slicing and serving.

Nutrition Information (per serving):

- Calories: 150
- Total Fat: 4g
- Saturated Fat: 0.5g
- Cholesterol: 0mg
- Sodium: 290mg
- Total Carbohydrate: 24g
- Dietary Fiber: 1g
- Sugars: 0.5g
- Protein: 4g

Feel free to adjust the seasoning or add more thyme and lemon zest to suit your taste preferences. Enjoy the delightful flavors of this Lemon Thyme Focaccia either as a standalone treat or paired with soups, salads, or as a side to your favorite dishes!

39. Caramel Apple Cinnamon Bread

Indulge in the cozy flavors of autumn with this delectable Caramel Apple Cinnamon Bread. Inspired by Gordon Ramsay's love for hearty, flavorful bread, this recipe combines the sweetness of caramel and the tartness of apples with warm cinnamon, creating a delightful treat perfect for any time of day.

Serving: Makes one loaf, serving approximately 10 slices.
Preparation Time: 15 minutes
Ready Time: 3 hours 30 minutes (including baking and cooling)

Ingredients:
- 1 cup warm water (110°F/43°C)
- 2 tablespoons vegetable oil
- 3 tablespoons caramel sauce
- 3 cups bread flour
- 1 teaspoon salt
- 2 tablespoons brown sugar
- 1 teaspoon ground cinnamon
- 2 1/4 teaspoons active dry yeast
- 1 cup diced apples (peeled and cored)

Instructions:

1. Begin by adding the warm water, vegetable oil, and caramel sauce to the bread machine pan.
2. In a separate bowl, combine the bread flour, salt, brown sugar, cinnamon, and active dry yeast. Add this dry mixture to the bread machine pan.
3. Select the "Dough" setting on your bread machine and start the cycle. Allow the machine to knead and mix the ingredients until a smooth dough forms. This process typically takes about 10-15 minutes.
4. Once the dough has been mixed and kneaded, add the diced apples to the dough. Close the bread machine and allow it to continue with its cycle, letting the apples incorporate evenly into the dough. This may take an additional 5-10 minutes.
5. After the cycle is complete, transfer the dough to a lightly floured surface. Shape it into a loaf and place it into a greased loaf pan.
6. Cover the loaf pan with a clean kitchen towel and let the dough rise in a warm, draft-free place for about 1-1.5 hours, or until it doubles in size.
7. Preheat your oven to 350°F (175°C). Once the dough has risen, bake it in the preheated oven for 25-30 minutes, or until the bread turns golden brown and sounds hollow when tapped on the bottom.
8. Remove the bread from the oven and allow it to cool in the pan for 10 minutes. Then, transfer the bread to a wire rack to cool completely before slicing.

Nutrition Information (per serving):
- Calories: 220
- Total Fat: 3g
- Saturated Fat: 0.5g
- Cholesterol: 0mg
- Sodium: 200mg
- Total Carbohydrate: 42g
- Dietary Fiber: 2g
- Sugars: 9g
- Protein: 5g

Enjoy this Caramel Apple Cinnamon Bread as a delightful breakfast or a sweet afternoon snack, perfect with a cup of tea or coffee!

40. Smoked Salmon and Dill Bagels

Delight your senses with a classic breakfast or brunch favorite, inspired by the culinary genius of Gordon Ramsay. These smoked salmon and dill bagels boast a harmonious blend of flavors and textures. The savory smoked salmon, paired with the aromatic dill and the satisfying chewiness of freshly baked bagels, creates a dish that is both elegant and comforting.

Serving: Makes 4 servings
Preparation Time: 15 minutes
Ready Time: 2 hours 30 minutes (including rising time)

Ingredients:
- For the Bagels:
- 1 cup warm water
- 2 1/4 teaspoons active dry yeast
- 3 tablespoons granulated sugar
- 3 cups bread flour
- 1 1/2 teaspoons salt
- 1 tablespoon olive oil
- 1 tablespoon honey
- 1 egg (for egg wash)
- Sesame seeds or poppy seeds (optional, for topping)
- For Assembly:
- 8 ounces smoked salmon
- 1/2 cup cream cheese, softened
- 2 tablespoons fresh dill, chopped
- Red onion slices (optional, for garnish)
- Capers (optional, for garnish)

Instructions:
1. Making the Bagel Dough:
- In the bread machine pan, combine warm water, yeast, and sugar. Let it sit for 5-10 minutes until it becomes frothy.
- Add bread flour, salt, olive oil, and honey to the yeast mixture in the bread machine pan.
- Select the dough cycle on the bread machine and start it. Allow the machine to knead and rise the dough.
2. Shaping and Boiling the Bagels:
- Once the dough cycle is complete, remove the dough from the machine and punch it down on a lightly floured surface.

- Divide the dough into 4 equal parts and shape each into a ball. Use your thumb to poke a hole through the center of each ball, shaping it into a bagel.
- Preheat your oven to 425°F (220°C). Bring a large pot of water to a gentle boil and carefully add the bagels, boiling them for 1-2 minutes per side.
- Remove the boiled bagels and place them on a baking sheet lined with parchment paper.

3. Baking the Bagels:
- Whisk the egg in a small bowl to make an egg wash. Brush the tops of the boiled bagels with the egg wash and sprinkle with sesame seeds or poppy seeds if desired.
- Bake the bagels in the preheated oven for 20-25 minutes or until they turn golden brown. Remove and let them cool on a wire rack.

4. Assembling the Bagels:
- Once the bagels have cooled, slice them in half horizontally.
- Spread a generous layer of softened cream cheese on the bottom half of each bagel.
- Top the cream cheese with smoked salmon slices and sprinkle with chopped fresh dill.
- If desired, add red onion slices and capers for additional flavor.

Nutrition Information (per serving):
- Calories: Approximately 450
- Total Fat: 14g
- Saturated Fat: 5g
- Cholesterol: 55mg
- Sodium: 1200mg
- Total Carbohydrates: 60g
- Dietary Fiber: 3g
- Total Sugars: 10g
- Protein: 20g

These smoked salmon and dill bagels are a luxurious treat perfect for a leisurely breakfast or a sophisticated brunch. Enjoy the blend of flavors and the satisfaction of homemade bagels, prepared effortlessly with the help of your trusty bread machine.

41. Date and Walnut Raisin Bread

Indulge in the delightful fusion of sweet and nutty flavors with our Date and Walnut Raisin Bread—a recipe inspired by the culinary genius of Gordon Ramsay. This aromatic bread, created exclusively for bread machines, combines the warmth of dates, the crunch of walnuts, and the natural sweetness of raisins, resulting in a perfect blend of textures and tastes. Elevate your baking experience with this easy-to-follow recipe that promises to bring a touch of Ramsay's expertise to your kitchen.

Serving: Yields one standard-sized loaf.
Preparation Time: 15 minutes
Ready Time: 3 hours (including rising and baking time)

Ingredients:
- 1 cup pitted dates, chopped
- 1/2 cup walnuts, chopped
- 1/2 cup raisins
- 1 1/4 cups warm water (about 110°F/43°C)
- 2 tablespoons olive oil
- 3 tablespoons honey
- 1 teaspoon salt
- 4 cups bread flour
- 1 1/2 teaspoons active dry yeast

Instructions:
1. Prepare Ingredients: Ensure the dates, walnuts, and raisins are chopped and ready for incorporation.
2. Load Bread Machine: In the bread machine pan, add the warm water, olive oil, honey, and salt.
3. Add Dry Ingredients: Place the bread flour on top of the wet ingredients, creating a mound. Make a small well in the center of the flour and add the yeast.
4. Layer Fruits and Nuts: Sprinkle the chopped dates, walnuts, and raisins evenly over the flour.
5. Set Bread Machine: Select the "Sweet" or "Fruit and Nut" setting on your bread machine. Choose the desired crust color and loaf size settings.
6. Start the Machine: Close the lid and start the bread machine. Allow it to complete the full cycle, including kneading, rising, and baking.

7. Cooling: Once the baking cycle is complete, carefully remove the bread from the machine and place it on a wire rack to cool.

8. Slice and Serve: Once cooled, slice the Date and Walnut Raisin Bread into thick, inviting slices. Serve with butter or cream cheese for an extra touch of indulgence.

Nutrition Information:
(Per serving, based on 12 slices)
- Calories: 230
- Total Fat: 7g
- Saturated Fat: 1g
- Trans Fat: 0g
- Cholesterol: 0mg
- Sodium: 200mg
- Total Carbohydrates: 38g
- Dietary Fiber: 2g
- Sugars: 11g
- Protein: 5g

Note: Nutrition information is approximate and may vary based on specific ingredients used.

42. Roasted Garlic and Parmesan Sourdough

Elevate your bread machine game with this exquisite Roasted Garlic and Parmesan Sourdough, inspired by the culinary genius of Gordon Ramsay. The aromatic blend of roasted garlic and the richness of Parmesan cheese create a symphony of flavors that will leave your taste buds delighted. Follow this simple yet sophisticated recipe to bring a touch of gourmet to your homemade bread.

Serving: Makes one delicious loaf, approximately 12 slices.
Preparation Time: 15 minutes
Ready Time: 3 hours (including rising and baking time)

Ingredients:
- 1 cup warm water (110°F/43°C)
- 2 tablespoons olive oil
- 1 teaspoon sugar

- 1 1/2 teaspoons salt
- 3 cups bread flour
- 2 teaspoons active dry yeast
- 1/2 cup grated Parmesan cheese
- 1 head of garlic
- Olive oil for roasting garlic
- Flour for dusting

Instructions:
1. Prepare Roasted Garlic:
- Preheat your oven to 400°F (200°C).
- Cut off the top of the garlic head to expose the cloves.
- Drizzle with olive oil, wrap in foil, and roast for 30-40 minutes or until cloves are soft and golden.
- Squeeze roasted garlic from the cloves and set aside.
2. Prepare Bread Machine:
- In the bread machine pan, combine warm water, olive oil, sugar, and salt.
3. Add Dry Ingredients:
- Add bread flour on top of the liquid ingredients, creating a mound.
- Make a well in the center of the flour and add the yeast.
4. Start the Machine:
- Place the bread machine pan into the bread machine and set it to the basic white bread setting.
5. Incorporate Garlic and Parmesan:
- When the machine signals for add-ins (usually during the second kneading cycle), add the grated Parmesan and the roasted garlic.
6. Allow the Machine to Finish:
- Let the bread machine complete the kneading, rising, and baking cycles.
7. Cool and Slice:
- Once the bread is done, carefully remove it from the machine and let it cool on a wire rack before slicing.
8. Enjoy:
- Serve slices on their own or with a drizzle of olive oil for an extra touch of luxury.

Nutrition Information:
Per Serving (1 slice)
- Calories: 150
- Total Fat: 5g

- Saturated Fat: 1.5g
- Trans Fat: 0g
- Cholesterol: 5mg
- Sodium: 280mg
- Total Carbohydrates: 21g
- Dietary Fiber: 1g
- Sugars: 0.5g
- Protein: 5g

Elevate your bread-making skills with this Gordon Ramsay-inspired Roasted Garlic and Parmesan Sourdough. Your kitchen will be filled with the irresistible aroma of freshly baked bread, and your taste buds will thank you for the gourmet experience.

43. Cheddar Jalapeño Beer Bread

Indulge your taste buds in the bold and flavorful world of bread-making with this Cheddar Jalapeño Beer Bread. Inspired by the culinary genius of Gordon Ramsay, this recipe adds a spicy kick and a cheesy twist to the classic beer bread. The marriage of sharp cheddar, zesty jalapeños, and the rich undertones of beer creates a loaf that's perfect for any occasion, whether it's a cozy family dinner or a gathering with friends.

Serving: Yields approximately 12 slices
Preparation Time: 15 minutes
Ready Time: 2 hours (including rise time)

Ingredients:
- 3 cups all-purpose flour
- 1 tablespoon baking powder
- 1 teaspoon salt
- 1/4 cup sugar
- 1 cup sharp cheddar cheese, shredded
- 1-2 jalapeños, finely diced (adjust to taste)
- 12 ounces beer (choose a flavorful ale or lager)
- 1/4 cup unsalted butter, melted

Instructions:

1. Preheat your bread machine according to the manufacturer's instructions.
2. In a large mixing bowl, whisk together the flour, baking powder, salt, and sugar.
3. Add the shredded cheddar cheese and diced jalapeños to the dry ingredients. Mix well to ensure an even distribution of cheese and jalapeños.
4. Pour in the beer and stir until just combined. Be careful not to overmix; a slightly lumpy batter is fine.
5. Transfer the batter to the preheated bread machine pan.
6. Set your bread machine to the "Quick Bread" or "Basic" cycle, ensuring it is set for a 2-pound loaf.
7. Once the mixing cycle is complete, brush the melted butter over the top of the batter.
8. Close the lid and allow the bread machine to continue with the baking cycle.
9. Once the bread is done baking, carefully remove it from the machine and let it cool on a wire rack for at least 15-20 minutes before slicing.

Nutrition Information:
(Per serving - 1 slice)
Calories: 210
Total Fat: 8g
Saturated Fat: 5g
Cholesterol: 20mg
Sodium: 380mg
Total Carbohydrates: 28g
Dietary Fiber: 1g
Sugars: 2g
Protein: 5g
Note: Nutritional values are approximate and may vary based on specific ingredients and serving sizes.

44. Olive and Herb Semolina Bread

Elevate your bread machine game with this Olive and Herb Semolina Bread, inspired by the culinary genius of Gordon Ramsay. The combination of earthy semolina, briny olives, and aromatic herbs creates a delightful symphony of flavors that will make this bread a standout in your repertoire. With the convenience of a bread machine, you can effortlessly achieve bakery-quality results that will impress even the most discerning palates.

Serving: Makes one 1.5-pound loaf (approximately 12 slices)
Preparation Time: 15 minutes
Ready Time: 3 hours

Ingredients:
- 1 cup warm water (about 110°F/43°C)
- 2 tablespoons olive oil
- 2 cups bread flour
- 1 cup semolina flour
- 1 teaspoon sugar
- 1 1/2 teaspoons salt
- 1 teaspoon dried oregano
- 1 teaspoon dried thyme
- 1 teaspoon dried rosemary
- 1/2 cup pitted Kalamata olives, chopped
- 2 teaspoons active dry yeast

Instructions:
1. Place the warm water, olive oil, bread flour, semolina flour, sugar, salt, oregano, thyme, and rosemary in the bread machine pan in the order recommended by the manufacturer.
2. Make a small well in the dry ingredients and add the chopped Kalamata olives.
3. In a corner of the pan, make a small indentation and add the yeast.
4. Place the bread machine pan into the bread machine, close the lid, and select the "Basic" or "White Bread" setting, depending on your machine.
5. Start the machine, and let it run through the entire cycle. The olives and herbs will be incorporated during the kneading process.
6. Once the baking cycle is complete, carefully remove the bread pan from the machine and let the bread cool in the pan for 10 minutes. Then transfer the loaf to a wire rack to cool completely.
7. Slice and serve this flavorful Olive and Herb Semolina Bread with your favorite spreads or alongside a hearty soup.

Nutrition Information:

Note: Nutritional values are approximate and may vary based on specific ingredients and serving sizes.
- Calories: 150 per slice (assuming 12 slices per loaf)
- Total Fat: 4g
- Saturated Fat: 0.5g
- Cholesterol: 0mg
- Sodium: 300mg
- Total Carbohydrates: 25g
- Dietary Fiber: 2g
- Sugars: 0.5g
- Protein: 4g

This Olive and Herb Semolina Bread is a delightful addition to your bread machine repertoire, marrying the convenience of modern technology with the timeless artistry of bread-making. Enjoy the delicious results inspired by the culinary expertise of Gordon Ramsay.

45. Cranberry Pecan Rye Bread

Elevate your bread machine repertoire with this delectable Cranberry Pecan Rye Bread inspired by the culinary genius of Gordon Ramsay. The perfect blend of tart cranberries, crunchy pecans, and the earthy tones of rye flour, this bread is a symphony of flavors that will tantalize your taste buds. Whether enjoyed on its own, toasted with a spread of butter, or as a complement to your favorite dishes, this bread is sure to become a staple in your kitchen.

Serving: 12 slices
Preparation Time: 15 minutes
Ready Time: 3 hours (including baking time)

Ingredients:
- 1 cup warm water (110°F/43°C)
- 2 tablespoons olive oil
- 3 tablespoons honey
- 1 cup rye flour
- 2 cups bread flour
- 1 teaspoon salt
- 1 ½ teaspoons active dry yeast

- ½ cup dried cranberries
- ½ cup chopped pecans

Instructions:
1. Prepare the Bread Machine:
- Place the warm water, olive oil, and honey in the bread machine pan.
2. Add Dry Ingredients:
- In a separate bowl, whisk together the rye flour, bread flour, and salt.
- Add the dry ingredients to the bread machine pan on top of the wet ingredients.
3. Create a Well:
- Make a well in the center of the flour mixture and add the yeast.
4. Start the Machine:
- Set your bread machine to the "Basic" or "Whole Wheat" setting, depending on your machine's options.
5. Incorporate Ingredients:
- Allow the machine to run until it prompts you to add additional ingredients (usually signaled by a beep). At this point, add the dried cranberries and chopped pecans.
6. Let the Machine Finish:
- Close the lid and let the bread machine complete its cycle. This will include kneading, rising, and baking.
7. Cool and Slice:
- Once the bread is done, carefully remove it from the machine and let it cool on a wire rack before slicing.
8. Enjoy:
- Serve the Cranberry Pecan Rye Bread on its own, with butter, or alongside your favorite dishes.

Nutrition Information:
Note: Nutritional values are approximate and may vary based on specific ingredients and serving sizes.
- Calories per serving: 180
- Total Fat: 6g
- Saturated Fat: 1g
- Trans Fat: 0g
- Cholesterol: 0mg
- Sodium: 200mg
- Total Carbohydrates: 29g
- Dietary Fiber: 3g

- Sugars: 7g
- Protein: 4g

Indulge in the delightful combination of cranberries and pecans in every bite of this Cranberry Pecan Rye Bread, a recipe that pays homage to the culinary expertise of Gordon Ramsay. Perfect for any occasion, this bread is a testament to the artistry of bread-making with the convenience of a bread machine.

46. Garlic Herb Pizza Dough

Elevate your pizza game with this delectable Garlic Herb Pizza Dough, inspired by the culinary genius of Gordon Ramsay. The aromatic blend of garlic and herbs transforms a simple pizza crust into a flavorful masterpiece. Prepare to delight your taste buds and impress your guests with this easy-to-follow bread machine recipe.

Serving: Makes 2 pizza crusts
Preparation Time: 15 minutes
Ready Time: 2 hours 15 minutes (includes rising time)

Ingredients:
- 1 cup warm water
- 2 tablespoons olive oil
- 3 cups all-purpose flour
- 1 teaspoon sugar
- 1 teaspoon salt
- 1 teaspoon garlic powder
- 1 teaspoon dried oregano
- 1 teaspoon dried basil
- 1 teaspoon dried thyme
- 1 1/2 teaspoons active dry yeast

Instructions:
1. Prepare the Bread Machine:
Place the warm water and olive oil into the bread machine pan.
2. Add Dry Ingredients:
In a separate bowl, combine the all-purpose flour, sugar, salt, garlic powder, dried oregano, dried basil, and dried thyme.

3. Layer the Ingredients:
Pour the dry ingredients on top of the wet ingredients in the bread machine pan, creating a mound. Make a well in the center of the dry ingredients and add the active dry yeast.

4. Start the Machine:
Insert the bread machine pan into the bread machine and select the dough setting. Start the machine, allowing it to mix and knead the dough.

5. Monitor the Dough:
Keep an eye on the dough as it mixes. If it appears too dry, add a tablespoon of water at a time. If it's too sticky, add a tablespoon of flour at a time.

6. Rising Time:
Once the dough cycle is complete, remove the dough from the machine and place it in a lightly oiled bowl. Cover with a damp cloth and let it rise in a warm place for about 1 hour, or until it has doubled in size.

7. Preheat the Oven:
Preheat your oven to 475°F (245°C). If you have a pizza stone, place it in the oven to heat.

8. Divide and Shape the Dough:
Punch down the risen dough and divide it into two equal portions. On a floured surface, roll out each portion into your desired pizza crust shape.

9. Add Toppings:
Transfer the pizza crusts to a pizza peel or baking sheet. Add your favorite pizza toppings.

10. Bake:
If using a pizza stone, carefully transfer the pizza to the preheated stone in the oven. Otherwise, place the baking sheet directly in the oven. Bake for 12-15 minutes or until the crust is golden brown and the toppings are bubbly.

11. Cool and Enjoy:
Allow the pizza to cool for a few minutes before slicing. Serve and savor the incredible flavors of your Garlic Herb Pizza Dough.

Nutrition Information:
(Per serving, based on 8 slices per pizza crust)
- Calories: 150
- Total Fat: 3g
- Saturated Fat: 0.5g
- Cholesterol: 0mg
- Sodium: 300mg

- Total Carbohydrates: 27g
- Dietary Fiber: 1g
- Sugars: 1g
- Protein: 4g

Note: Nutritional values may vary depending on specific ingredients and toppings used.

47. Roasted Beet and Goat Cheese Bread

Elevate your bread machine experience with the delectable fusion of earthy roasted beets and creamy goat cheese in this unique and flavorful Roasted Beet and Goat Cheese Bread. Inspired by the culinary genius of Gordon Ramsay, this recipe promises to tantalize your taste buds with every bite. The beautiful hues of the beets and the richness of the goat cheese make this bread a visually stunning and delicious addition to your baking repertoire.

Serving: 8-10 slices
Preparation Time: 20 minutes
Ready Time: 3 hours

Ingredients:
- 1 cup roasted beets, finely diced
- 4 oz goat cheese, crumbled
- 1 1/2 cups bread flour
- 1 cup whole wheat flour
- 1 tablespoon sugar
- 1 teaspoon salt
- 1 packet (2 1/4 teaspoons) active dry yeast
- 1 cup warm water (110°F/43°C)
- 2 tablespoons olive oil
- 1 tablespoon honey
- Extra flour for dusting

Instructions:
1. In a small bowl, dissolve the sugar in warm water and sprinkle the yeast over the top. Allow it to sit for about 5 minutes until it becomes frothy.

2. In a large mixing bowl, combine the bread flour, whole wheat flour, and salt.
3. Make a well in the center of the dry ingredients and pour in the yeast mixture, olive oil, and honey. Mix until a dough forms.
4. Turn the dough onto a floured surface and knead for about 8-10 minutes or until it becomes smooth and elastic.
5. Place the dough in a lightly oiled bowl, cover it with a clean kitchen towel, and let it rise in a warm place for about 1-2 hours or until it has doubled in size.
6. Preheat your oven to 375°F (190°C).
7. Punch down the risen dough and incorporate the roasted beets and crumbled goat cheese, kneading until they are evenly distributed.
8. Shape the dough into a round or oval loaf and place it on a parchment-lined baking sheet. Let it rise for an additional 30-45 minutes.
9. Bake in the preheated oven for 25-30 minutes or until the bread is golden brown and sounds hollow when tapped on the bottom.
10. Allow the bread to cool on a wire rack before slicing.

Nutrition Information:
(Per serving - based on 8 servings)
- Calories: 240
- Total Fat: 7g
- Saturated Fat: 3g
- Trans Fat: 0g
- Cholesterol: 10mg
- Sodium: 350mg
- Total Carbohydrates: 38g
- Dietary Fiber: 4g
- Sugars: 5g
- Protein: 8g

Enjoy this Roasted Beet and Goat Cheese Bread as a standalone treat, or pair it with your favorite soups and salads for a delightful and satisfying meal.

48. Dark Chocolate Cherry Sourdough

Indulge your senses in a symphony of rich flavors with our Dark Chocolate Cherry Sourdough, a delightful creation inspired by the culinary genius of Gordon Ramsay. This unique bread machine recipe combines the earthy tang of sourdough with the decadence of dark chocolate and the sweet burst of cherries. Elevate your baking experience with this gourmet treat that effortlessly marries the expertise of a master chef with the ease of your trusty bread machine.

Serving: Makes one loaf (approximately 12 slices)
Preparation Time: 15 minutes
Ready Time: 3 hours and 30 minutes (including rising and baking time)

Ingredients:
- 1 cup active sourdough starter
- 1 1/2 cups bread flour
- 1 1/2 cups whole wheat flour
- 1 teaspoon salt
- 1/4 cup honey
- 1/4 cup olive oil
- 1/2 cup dark chocolate chips
- 1/2 cup dried cherries, chopped
- 3/4 cup warm water

Instructions:
1. In the bread machine pan, combine the active sourdough starter, bread flour, whole wheat flour, salt, honey, and olive oil.
2. Add the dark chocolate chips and chopped dried cherries to the mixture.
3. Gradually add warm water to the pan while the bread machine is running, allowing the dough to come together. Adjust the water as needed to achieve a smooth and slightly sticky dough consistency.
4. Set the bread machine to the "Dough" setting and let it run through the kneading and rising cycles.
5. Once the dough cycle is complete, transfer the dough to a floured surface and shape it into a loaf.
6. Place the shaped dough into a greased or parchment-lined loaf pan.
7. Allow the dough to rise in a warm place for approximately 1-2 hours or until it doubles in size.
8. Preheat your oven to 375°F (190°C).
9. Bake the loaf for 30-35 minutes or until the top is golden brown and the bread sounds hollow when tapped.

10. Allow the Dark Chocolate Cherry Sourdough to cool in the pan for 10 minutes before transferring it to a wire rack to cool completely.

Nutrition Information:
(Per slice, assuming 12 slices)
- Calories: 220
- Total Fat: 8g
- Saturated Fat: 2g
- Trans Fat: 0g
- Cholesterol: 0mg
- Sodium: 200mg
- Total Carbohydrates: 32g
- Dietary Fiber: 3g
- Sugars: 8g
- Protein: 5g

Note: Nutrition information is approximate and may vary based on specific ingredients used.

49. Tomato Basil Parmesan Focaccia

Elevate your bread machine game with this delightful Tomato Basil Parmesan Focaccia inspired by the culinary genius of Gordon Ramsay. The combination of juicy tomatoes, fragrant basil, and savory Parmesan cheese creates a flavor symphony that will leave your taste buds singing. Perfect for sharing with loved ones or savoring on your own, this focaccia is a testament to the artistry of bread making.

Serving: Makes one 9-inch round focaccia; approximately 8 servings.
Preparation Time: 15 minutes
Ready Time: 2 hours (including rise time)

Ingredients:
- 1 cup warm water (110°F/43°C)
- 2 tablespoons olive oil
- 3 cups bread flour
- 1 teaspoon sugar
- 1 teaspoon salt
- 1 tablespoon dried basil

- 1 teaspoon garlic powder
- 1 packet (2 1/4 teaspoons) active dry yeast
- 1 cup cherry tomatoes, halved
- 1/2 cup grated Parmesan cheese
- Extra olive oil for drizzling
- Fresh basil leaves for garnish (optional)

Instructions:
1. Prepare the Bread Machine:
Place the warm water, olive oil, bread flour, sugar, salt, dried basil, garlic powder, and active dry yeast in the bread machine pan in the order recommended by the manufacturer.
2. Select the Dough Setting:
Set your bread machine to the dough setting and start the cycle. Allow the machine to knead and rise the dough.
3. Preheat the Oven:
Preheat your oven to 400°F (200°C) during the last 15 minutes of the dough cycle.
4. Prepare the Focaccia:
Once the dough cycle is complete, transfer the dough to a lightly floured surface. Roll it out into a 9-inch round and place it on a parchment-lined baking sheet.
5. Add Toppings:
Press halved cherry tomatoes into the dough, sprinkle with grated Parmesan cheese, and drizzle with olive oil.
6. Final Rise:
Allow the topped dough to rest and rise for an additional 15-20 minutes.
7. Bake:
Bake in the preheated oven for 20-25 minutes or until the focaccia is golden brown and sounds hollow when tapped on the bottom.
8. Cool and Garnish:
Allow the focaccia to cool on a wire rack. Garnish with fresh basil leaves if desired.

Nutrition Information:
Note: Nutrition values are approximate and may vary based on specific ingredients used.
- Serving Size: 1 slice (assuming 8 slices)
- Calories: 220
- Total Fat: 7g

- Saturated Fat: 2g
- Cholesterol: 5mg
- Sodium: 400mg
- Total Carbohydrates: 32g
- Dietary Fiber: 2g
- Sugars: 1g
- Protein: 8g

Enjoy this Tomato Basil Parmesan Focaccia as a delightful accompaniment to meals or as a stand-alone treat. With the ease of your bread machine and the inspiration of Gordon Ramsay, you'll have a masterpiece in every slice.

50. Cinnamon Swirl Pumpkin Bread

Indulge in the warm embrace of autumn with this delightful Cinnamon Swirl Pumpkin Bread—a delectable creation inspired by the culinary genius of Gordon Ramsay. Immerse yourself in the comforting aroma of cinnamon and the rich, earthy notes of pumpkin. This recipe beautifully combines the ease of a bread machine with the exquisite flavors that only the Ramsay touch can provide. Elevate your baking game and savor every slice of this seasonal delight!

Serving: Yields approximately 12 slices
Preparation Time: 15 minutes
Ready Time: 3 hours 30 minutes

Ingredients:
- 1 cup canned pumpkin puree
- 1/2 cup vegetable oil
- 2 large eggs
- 1 teaspoon vanilla extract
- 1/2 cup granulated sugar
- 1/2 cup brown sugar, packed
- 2 cups all-purpose flour
- 1 teaspoon baking powder
- 1/2 teaspoon baking soda
- 1/2 teaspoon salt
- 1 teaspoon ground cinnamon

- 1/2 teaspoon ground nutmeg
- 1/4 teaspoon ground cloves
- 1/4 teaspoon ground ginger

For the Cinnamon Swirl:
- 1/3 cup granulated sugar
- 1 tablespoon ground cinnamon

Instructions:
1. In the bread machine pan, combine the pumpkin puree, vegetable oil, eggs, and vanilla extract. Add the granulated sugar and brown sugar, ensuring a smooth and well-incorporated mixture.
2. In a separate bowl, whisk together the all-purpose flour, baking powder, baking soda, salt, cinnamon, nutmeg, cloves, and ginger.
3. Gradually add the dry ingredients to the wet ingredients in the bread machine pan. Set the bread machine to the "dough" setting and allow it to knead and rise.
4. Meanwhile, prepare the cinnamon swirl mixture by combining the granulated sugar and ground cinnamon in a small bowl.
5. Once the dough cycle is complete, turn the dough out onto a floured surface. Roll it into a rectangle and evenly spread the cinnamon swirl mixture over the dough.
6. Starting from one end, tightly roll the dough into a log. Place the rolled dough into a greased loaf pan, cover it with a clean kitchen towel, and let it rise for an additional 1-2 hours, or until it doubles in size.
7. Preheat the oven to 350°F (175°C). Bake the pumpkin bread for 30-35 minutes, or until the top is golden brown, and a toothpick inserted into the center comes out clean.
8. Allow the bread to cool in the pan for 10 minutes before transferring it to a wire rack to cool completely.

Nutrition Information:
(Per serving, based on 12 servings)
- Calories: 230
- Total Fat: 10g
- Saturated Fat: 1.5g
- Cholesterol: 31mg
- Sodium: 180mg
- Total Carbohydrates: 34g
- Dietary Fiber: 1g
- Sugars: 16g

- Protein: 3g

Embrace the warmth of fall with every slice of this Cinnamon Swirl Pumpkin Bread—a delightful creation that seamlessly blends the convenience of a bread machine with the culinary expertise inspired by Gordon Ramsay.

51. Three Cheese Rosemary Baguette

Indulge your taste buds in the delightful harmony of flavors with our Three Cheese Rosemary Baguette—a culinary masterpiece inspired by the renowned Gordon Ramsay. This artisanal bread, prepared effortlessly in your bread machine, combines the richness of three distinct cheeses and the aromatic essence of fresh rosemary, delivering a sensory experience that elevates the art of home baking. Impress your guests or savor it on your own—this recipe promises to be a highlight in your culinary repertoire.

Serving: Yields one savory Three Cheese Rosemary Baguette, approximately 12 slices.
Preparation Time: 15 minutes
Ready Time: 3 hours (including rising and baking time)

Ingredients:
- 1 cup warm water (110°F/43°C)
- 2 tablespoons olive oil
- 3 cups all-purpose flour
- 1 teaspoon salt
- 1 tablespoon sugar
- 2 teaspoons active dry yeast
- 1 cup shredded mozzarella cheese
- 1/2 cup crumbled feta cheese
- 1/2 cup grated Parmesan cheese
- 2 tablespoons fresh rosemary, finely chopped

Instructions:
1. Begin by placing the warm water, olive oil, flour, salt, sugar, and active dry yeast into the bread machine in the order recommended by the manufacturer.

2. Select the dough cycle on your bread machine and start the process. Allow the machine to mix and knead the ingredients until a smooth and elastic dough forms.
3. Once the dough cycle is complete, transfer the dough to a floured surface. Roll it out into a rectangle, approximately 12 inches by 8 inches.
4. Sprinkle the mozzarella, feta, Parmesan, and chopped rosemary evenly over the dough.
5. Roll the dough tightly from the longer side, forming a log-shaped baguette. Pinch the seams to seal.
6. Place the rolled dough on a parchment-lined baking sheet. Cover it with a clean kitchen towel and let it rise in a warm place for about 1-1.5 hours, or until it doubles in size.
7. Preheat your oven to 375°F (190°C) during the last 15 minutes of the rising time.
8. Bake the risen baguette in the preheated oven for 25-30 minutes or until golden brown and sounds hollow when tapped.
9. Allow the Three Cheese Rosemary Baguette to cool for a few minutes before slicing and serving.

Nutrition Information:
Note: Nutrition values are approximate and may vary based on specific ingredients used.
- Calories: 220 per slice
- Total Fat: 9g
- Saturated Fat: 4g
- Cholesterol: 20mg
- Sodium: 380mg
- Total Carbohydrates: 27g
- Dietary Fiber: 1g
- Sugars: 1g
- Protein: 8g

Enjoy the delightful blend of cheeses and fragrant rosemary in every bite of this exquisite baguette!

52. Orange Cranberry Walnut Bread

Indulge your taste buds with the delightful fusion of citrusy zest, tart cranberries, and crunchy walnuts in this Orange Cranberry Walnut

Bread. Inspired by the culinary brilliance of Gordon Ramsay, this bread machine recipe promises a symphony of flavors and textures that will elevate your baking experience. Perfect for breakfast, brunch, or as a sweet treat any time of the day, this bread is a testament to the harmonious marriage of simple ingredients and expert technique.

Serving: Makes one loaf, approximately 12 slices.
Preparation Time: 15 minutes
Ready Time: 3 hours (including rising and baking time)

Ingredients:
- 1 cup orange juice (freshly squeezed for optimal flavor)
- Zest of 1 large orange
- 2 tablespoons unsalted butter, softened
- 3 cups all-purpose flour
- 1/2 cup granulated sugar
- 1 teaspoon salt
- 1 1/2 teaspoons active dry yeast
- 1/2 cup dried cranberries
- 1/2 cup chopped walnuts

Instructions:
1. Place the orange juice, orange zest, and softened butter in the bread machine pan.
2. In a separate bowl, whisk together the flour, sugar, and salt until well combined.
3. Add the dry ingredients to the bread machine pan, creating a layer on top of the wet ingredients.
4. Make a small well in the center of the dry ingredients and add the yeast.
5. Select the "Sweet Bread" or equivalent setting on your bread machine.
6. Close the lid and start the machine.
7. When the machine signals the addition of mix-ins (usually during the kneading cycle), add the dried cranberries and chopped walnuts.
8. Close the lid and allow the bread machine to complete the cycle.
9. Once the baking cycle is finished, carefully remove the bread from the machine and let it cool on a wire rack before slicing.

Nutrition Information:
(Per slice - assuming 12 slices)

- Calories: 230
- Total Fat: 7g
- Saturated Fat: 2.5g
- Cholesterol: 10mg
- Sodium: 180mg
- Total Carbohydrates: 38g
- Dietary Fiber: 2g
- Sugars: 12g
- Protein: 4g

Note: Nutrition information may vary based on specific ingredient brands and quantities used. Adjustments can be made for dietary preferences and restrictions.

53. Brown Butter Sage Pretzel Bites

Elevate your bread machine game with these delectable Brown Butter Sage Pretzel Bites inspired by the culinary genius, Gordon Ramsay. The rich flavors of browned butter and aromatic sage come together to create bite-sized pieces of heaven that are perfect for any occasion. These pretzel bites are a delightful blend of savory and buttery goodness, sure to impress even the most discerning palates.

Serving: Makes approximately 48 pretzel bites.
Preparation Time: 20 minutes
Ready Time: 2 hours (including rising time)

Ingredients:
- 1 1/2 cups warm water
- 1 tablespoon sugar
- 2 teaspoons active dry yeast
- 4 cups all-purpose flour
- 1 teaspoon salt
- 1/4 cup unsalted butter, melted
- 1/4 cup baking soda
- 2 tablespoons fresh sage, finely chopped
- 1/2 cup unsalted butter, for browning
- Coarse sea salt, for sprinkling

Instructions:

1. Activate the Yeast:

In a bowl, combine warm water and sugar. Sprinkle the yeast over the mixture and let it sit for 5-10 minutes until it becomes foamy.

2. Prepare the Dough:

In a large bowl, combine the flour and salt. Pour in the melted butter and activated yeast mixture. Mix until the dough comes together. Knead the dough on a floured surface until it becomes smooth and elastic.

3. First Rise:

Place the dough in a lightly oiled bowl, cover it with a clean kitchen towel, and let it rise in a warm place for about 1 hour or until it doubles in size.

4. Preheat and Shape:

Preheat your bread machine to the dough setting. Once the dough has risen, punch it down and divide it into small portions. Roll each portion into a rope and cut into bite-sized pieces.

5. Boil the Pretzel Bites:

In a large pot, bring water to a boil. Add the baking soda and boil the pretzel bites in batches for about 30 seconds. Remove with a slotted spoon and place on a parchment-lined baking sheet.

6. Brown Butter Sage Sauce:

In a skillet over medium heat, melt the 1/2 cup of butter. Add the chopped sage and cook until the butter turns golden brown and the sage is fragrant.

7. Bake:

Preheat your oven to 425°F (220°C). Brush the pretzel bites with the brown butter sage sauce and sprinkle with coarse sea salt. Bake for 12-15 minutes or until golden brown.

8. Serve:

Allow the pretzel bites to cool slightly before serving. Enjoy them on their own or with your favorite dipping sauce.

Nutrition Information:

(Per serving, based on 4 pretzel bites)
- Calories: 180
- Fat: 8g
- Saturated Fat: 5g
- Cholesterol: 20mg
- Sodium: 300mg
- Carbohydrates: 23g

- Fiber: 1g
- Sugars: 1g
- Protein: 3g

Note: Nutrition information is approximate and may vary based on specific ingredients used.

54. Parmesan Black Pepper Grissini

Elevate your bread machine game with these Parmesan Black Pepper Grissini, inspired by the culinary genius of Gordon Ramsay. These crispy and flavorful breadsticks are the perfect addition to any meal or a delightful snack on their own. The combination of nutty Parmesan and the kick of black pepper creates a taste sensation that will leave your taste buds wanting more. Impress your guests or simply treat yourself to these artisanal delights that bring the essence of Ramsay's expertise into your home kitchen.

Serving: Makes approximately 24 grissini
Preparation Time: 15 minutes
Ready Time: 2 hours (includes rising time)

Ingredients:
- 1 cup warm water (110°F/43°C)
- 2 tablespoons olive oil
- 1 teaspoon honey
- 3 cups bread flour
- 1 teaspoon salt
- 1 teaspoon black pepper, freshly ground
- 1 cup Parmesan cheese, finely grated
- 1 packet (2 1/4 teaspoons) active dry yeast
- Cornmeal for dusting

Instructions:
1. Prepare the Bread Machine:
Place the warm water, olive oil, and honey in the bread machine pan.
2. Add Dry Ingredients:

On top of the wet ingredients, add the bread flour, salt, black pepper, Parmesan cheese, and active dry yeast. Make sure the yeast doesn't directly contact the salt.

3. Set the Bread Machine:

Set your bread machine to the "Dough" or "Pizza Dough" setting and start the cycle. Allow the machine to mix and knead the ingredients until a smooth, elastic dough forms.

4. Rising Time:

Once the dough cycle is complete, let the dough rise in the bread machine for an additional 1 hour, or until it has doubled in size.

5. Preheat Oven:

Preheat your oven to 375°F (190°C). Line baking sheets with parchment paper and sprinkle with cornmeal.

6. Shape Grissini:

Turn the dough out onto a lightly floured surface. Divide it into 24 equal portions. Roll each portion into a thin rope, about 10-12 inches long. Place the ropes on the prepared baking sheets.

7. Bake:

Bake the grissini in the preheated oven for 12-15 minutes or until golden brown and crisp.

8. Cool:

Allow the grissini to cool on the baking sheets for a few minutes before transferring them to a wire rack to cool completely.

9. Serve:

Serve the Parmesan Black Pepper Grissini as a side to soups, salads, or enjoy them on their own as a delightful snack.

Nutrition Information:
(Per serving - 2 grissini)
- Calories: 120
- Total Fat: 4g
- Saturated Fat: 1.5g
- Trans Fat: 0g
- Cholesterol: 5mg
- Sodium: 180mg
- Total Carbohydrates: 16g
- Dietary Fiber: 1g
- Sugars: 0.5g
- Protein: 4g

Note: Nutrition information is approximate and may vary based on specific ingredients used.

55. Fig and Prosciutto Fougasse

Indulge your taste buds in a symphony of flavors with our Fig and Prosciutto Fougasse, a delightful bread creation inspired by the culinary genius of Gordon Ramsay. This artisanal bread, with its soft interior and golden crust, is adorned with the sweet allure of figs and the savory richness of prosciutto. Perfect for any occasion, this recipe combines the convenience of a bread machine with the exquisite touch of a master chef.

Serving: Makes one large Fougasse
Preparation Time: 15 minutes
Ready Time: 3 hours (including rising and baking time)

Ingredients:
- 1 cup warm water
- 2 tablespoons olive oil
- 1 teaspoon salt
- 3 cups bread flour
- 1 tablespoon sugar
- 1 ½ teaspoons active dry yeast
- ½ cup dried figs, chopped
- 4 slices prosciutto, thinly sliced
- 1 tablespoon fresh rosemary, chopped
- Olive oil, for brushing

Instructions:
1. Prepare the Bread Machine:
Place the warm water, olive oil, salt, bread flour, sugar, and active dry yeast in the bread machine in the order recommended by the manufacturer.
2. Select the Dough Setting:
Choose the dough setting on your bread machine and start the cycle. Allow the machine to knead and rise the dough.
3. Add Figs and Prosciutto:

When the dough cycle is complete, remove the dough and place it on a floured surface. Gently knead in the chopped figs and half of the sliced prosciutto.

4. Shape the Fougasse:

Roll out the dough into a large oval shape. With a knife or scissors, make several diagonal cuts on each side of the oval, leaving a wide strip down the center. Pull the cut sections outward to create a leaf-like shape.

5. Final Rise:

Place the shaped fougasse on a baking sheet lined with parchment paper. Cover it with a kitchen towel and let it rise for about 30 minutes.

6. Preheat the Oven:

Preheat your oven to 400°F (200°C).

7. Brush with Olive Oil:

Brush the fougasse with olive oil and sprinkle the remaining prosciutto and chopped rosemary on top.

8. Bake:

Bake in the preheated oven for 20-25 minutes or until the bread is golden brown and sounds hollow when tapped on the bottom.

9. Cool and Serve:

Allow the fougasse to cool on a wire rack for a few minutes before slicing. Serve warm and enjoy the delightful combination of figs, prosciutto, and rosemary.

Nutrition Information:

Note: Nutrition values are approximate and may vary based on specific ingredients used.
- Serving Size: 1 slice
- Calories: 150
- Total Fat: 5g
- Saturated Fat: 1g
- Cholesterol: 5mg
- Sodium: 200mg
- Total Carbohydrates: 23g
- Dietary Fiber: 2g
- Sugars: 4g
- Protein: 5g

Indulge in the sophistication of this Fig and Prosciutto Fougasse, a bread that effortlessly combines the rustic charm of a traditional fougasse with the gourmet touch inspired by the renowned Gordon Ramsay.

56. Cardamom Orange Blossom Brioche

Elevate your bread machine repertoire with the tantalizing blend of fragrant cardamom and delicate orange blossom in this Cardamom Orange Blossom Brioche. Inspired by the culinary genius of Gordon Ramsay, this recipe combines the warmth of cardamom, the floral notes of orange blossom, and the irresistible fluffiness of brioche. Perfect for a luxurious breakfast or a delightful afternoon treat, this bread will surely become a favorite in your home.

Serving: Makes 1 loaf
Preparation Time: 15 minutes
Ready Time: 3 hours (including rising time)

Ingredients:
- 1 cup warm milk
- 1/2 cup unsalted butter, softened
- 1/4 cup granulated sugar
- 3 large eggs
- 4 cups all-purpose flour
- 1 teaspoon salt
- 2 teaspoons active dry yeast
- 1 teaspoon ground cardamom
- 1 tablespoon orange blossom water

Instructions:
1. Place the warm milk, softened butter, granulated sugar, and eggs in the bread machine pan in the order recommended by the manufacturer.
2. In a separate bowl, whisk together the flour and salt. Add this dry mixture on top of the wet ingredients in the bread machine pan.
3. Make a small well in the center of the flour mixture and add the active dry yeast. Sprinkle the ground cardamom over the yeast.
4. Set the bread machine to the "dough" cycle and start the machine. Allow it to mix and knead the dough until it's smooth and elastic.
5. Once the dough cycle is complete, transfer the dough to a floured surface. Knead the dough a few times and then shape it into a loaf.

6. Place the shaped dough into a greased loaf pan, cover it with a clean kitchen towel, and let it rise in a warm place for about 1-2 hours, or until it doubles in size.
7. Preheat the oven to 350°F (175°C). Brush the top of the risen dough with orange blossom water for a subtle floral aroma.
8. Bake the brioche in the preheated oven for 25-30 minutes or until the top is golden brown and the bread sounds hollow when tapped.
9. Allow the brioche to cool in the pan for 10 minutes, then transfer it to a wire rack to cool completely.

Nutrition Information:
(Per Serving)
- Calories: 220
- Total Fat: 8g
- Saturated Fat: 5g
- Cholesterol: 55mg
- Sodium: 200mg
- Total Carbohydrates: 31g
- Dietary Fiber: 1g
- Sugars: 5g
- Protein: 5g

Enjoy the delightful Cardamom Orange Blossom Brioche with your favorite spread or as a standalone treat. This aromatic bread is sure to captivate your taste buds and impress anyone lucky enough to enjoy it.

57. Stout and Cheddar Beer Bread

Elevate your bread machine game with this robust and flavorful Stout and Cheddar Beer Bread inspired by the culinary genius of Gordon Ramsay. The rich combination of dark stout and sharp cheddar creates a hearty and satisfying loaf that's perfect for any occasion. Let your bread machine do the work while you enjoy the delightful aroma filling your kitchen.

Serving: Makes one 2-pound loaf, approximately 12 slices.
Preparation Time: 15 minutes
Ready Time: 3 hours 30 minutes

Ingredients:
- 1 cup stout beer (room temperature)
- 1/2 cup water (room temperature)
- 1 tablespoon olive oil
- 3 cups bread flour
- 1 cup shredded sharp cheddar cheese
- 2 tablespoons sugar
- 1 teaspoon salt
- 2 1/4 teaspoons active dry yeast

Instructions:
1. Place the stout beer, water, and olive oil into the bread machine pan.
2. In a separate bowl, combine the bread flour, shredded cheddar cheese, sugar, and salt. Add this mixture to the bread machine pan.
3. Make a small well in the dry ingredients and add the active dry yeast to it, ensuring it does not come into direct contact with the liquid.
4. Place the bread machine pan into the bread machine, and select the "Basic" or "White Bread" setting, depending on your machine's options. Choose the 2-pound loaf size and start the machine.
5. Allow the bread machine to complete the full cycle, including the rising and baking phases. This typically takes about 3 hours.
6. Once the cycle is complete, carefully remove the bread pan from the machine and transfer the loaf onto a wire rack to cool.
7. Allow the Stout and Cheddar Beer Bread to cool for at least 30 minutes before slicing.

Nutrition Information (per serving):
- Calories: 220
- Total Fat: 7g
- Saturated Fat: 3.5g
- Cholesterol: 15mg
- Sodium: 280mg
- Total Carbohydrates: 29g
- Dietary Fiber: 1g
- Sugars: 2g
- Protein: 8g

Note: Nutrition information is approximate and may vary based on specific ingredients and serving sizes.

58. Sun-dried Tomato Pesto Bread

Elevate your bread machine experience with this delectable Sun-dried Tomato Pesto Bread inspired by the culinary genius of Gordon Ramsay. Bursting with vibrant flavors, this bread is a celebration of sun-dried tomatoes, fragrant pesto, and the irresistible aroma of freshly baked bread. Whether you're a seasoned baker or a novice, this recipe promises a delightful journey for your taste buds.

Serving: Makes 1 loaf
Preparation Time: 15 minutes
Ready Time: 3 hours (including rising and baking)

Ingredients:
- 1 cup warm water
- 2 tablespoons olive oil
- 3 cups bread flour
- 1 teaspoon sugar
- 1 teaspoon salt
- 2 teaspoons active dry yeast
- 1/2 cup sun-dried tomatoes, chopped
- 1/4 cup pesto sauce

Instructions:
1. In the bread machine pan, combine warm water and olive oil.
2. Add bread flour, sugar, and salt to the pan, ensuring the dry ingredients cover the liquid.
3. Make a small well in the center of the dry ingredients and add the active dry yeast.
4. Select the "Dough" setting on your bread machine and let it run its cycle, allowing the machine to mix and knead the dough. This typically takes about 1.5 to 2 hours.
5. Once the dough cycle is complete, transfer the dough to a floured surface and gently knead in the chopped sun-dried tomatoes and pesto until evenly distributed.
6. Shape the dough into a loaf and place it in a greased or parchment-lined loaf pan.
7. Cover the pan with a clean kitchen towel and let the dough rise in a warm place for about 1 hour, or until it doubles in size.
8. Preheat your oven to 375°F (190°C).

9. Bake the bread in the preheated oven for 25-30 minutes or until the top is golden brown, and the loaf sounds hollow when tapped.
10. Allow the bread to cool in the pan for 10 minutes before transferring it to a wire rack to cool completely.

Nutrition Information:
Note: Nutrition values are approximate and may vary based on specific ingredients used.
- Calories: 180 per serving (1 slice)
- Total Fat: 5g
- Saturated Fat: 1g
- Trans Fat: 0g
- Cholesterol: 0mg
- Sodium: 250mg
- Total Carbohydrates: 30g
- Dietary Fiber: 2g
- Sugars: 2g
- Protein: 5g

Indulge in the savory goodness of this Sun-dried Tomato Pesto Bread, a perfect blend of simplicity and sophistication that will leave your kitchen smelling like a five-star restaurant. Enjoy it fresh out of the oven or toasted with a slather of butter for a truly memorable experience.

59. Hazelnut Espresso Chocolate Loaf

Indulge in the decadent world of artisanal bread-making with a touch of culinary genius inspired by none other than Gordon Ramsay. This Hazelnut Espresso Chocolate Loaf is a delightful fusion of rich flavors, combining the robust essence of espresso, the nutty crunch of hazelnuts, and the velvety goodness of chocolate. Elevate your bread machine repertoire and awaken your taste buds to a symphony of textures and tastes.

Serving: 1 loaf (approximately 12 slices)
Preparation Time: 15 minutes
Ready Time: 3 hours (including rising and baking)

Ingredients:

- 1 cup warm water (110°F/43°C)
- 2 tablespoons instant espresso powder
- 3 tablespoons honey
- 1 1/2 teaspoons active dry yeast
- 3 cups bread flour
- 1/4 cup unsweetened cocoa powder
- 1 teaspoon salt
- 1/2 cup chopped hazelnuts, toasted
- 1/2 cup semisweet chocolate chips
- 2 tablespoons olive oil
- Cooking spray (for greasing)

Instructions:
1. In a small bowl, combine warm water and instant espresso powder. Stir until the espresso powder is fully dissolved. Add honey and sprinkle the active dry yeast over the mixture. Let it sit for 5-10 minutes until the yeast is frothy.
2. In the bread machine pan, combine bread flour, cocoa powder, and salt. Pour the espresso mixture over the dry ingredients.
3. Add chopped hazelnuts, semisweet chocolate chips, and olive oil to the bread machine pan.
4. Place the pan into the bread machine, select the "Basic" or "Sweet" setting, and choose the desired crust color. Start the machine.
5. Allow the bread machine to complete the cycle, including the rising and baking phases. This typically takes about 3 hours.
6. Once the baking is complete, carefully remove the hazelnut espresso chocolate loaf from the bread machine pan and place it on a wire rack to cool.
7. Allow the loaf to cool completely before slicing.

Nutrition Information:
Note: Nutritional values are approximate and may vary based on specific ingredients and serving sizes.
- Calories per serving: 220
- Total Fat: 9g
- Saturated Fat: 2g
- Trans Fat: 0g
- Cholesterol: 0mg
- Sodium: 170mg
- Total Carbohydrates: 32g

- Dietary Fiber: 3g
- Sugars: 6g
- Protein: 5g

Immerse yourself in the divine aroma and rich flavors of this Hazelnut Espresso Chocolate Loaf—a testament to the culinary expertise that is Gordon Ramsay-inspired bread-making.

60. Caramelized Onion and Gruyere Boule

Elevate your bread machine game with this delectable Caramelized Onion and Gruyere Boule inspired by the culinary genius of Gordon Ramsay. The rich flavors of sweet caramelized onions and the nutty goodness of Gruyere cheese come together in a perfect harmony, creating a bread that's not only a joy to make but also a delight to savor. Get ready to impress your taste buds and guests with this savory masterpiece!

Serving: Makes one large boule, approximately 12 slices.
Preparation Time: 15 minutes
Ready Time: 3 hours (including rise time)

Ingredients:
- 1 cup finely chopped onions
- 2 tablespoons olive oil
- 1 teaspoon sugar
- 1 1/2 cups warm water
- 3 1/4 cups bread flour
- 2 teaspoons active dry yeast
- 1 teaspoon salt
- 1 cup shredded Gruyere cheese
- 1 tablespoon dried thyme (optional, for added flavor)

Instructions:
1. Caramelize the Onions:
- In a skillet, heat the olive oil over medium heat.
- Add the chopped onions and sugar, sautéing until the onions turn golden brown and caramelized. Set aside to cool.
2. Prepare the Dough:

- In the bread machine pan, combine warm water, bread flour, yeast, and salt.
- Select the dough setting and let the bread machine work its magic.

3. Incorporate the Goodness:
- Once the dough has risen, transfer it to a floured surface.
- Flatten the dough and spread the caramelized onions, Gruyere cheese, and dried thyme evenly over the surface.
- Roll the dough into a log and place it in a greased and floured round baking pan.

4. Second Rise:
- Cover the pan with a clean kitchen towel and let the dough rise for another hour or until doubled in size.

5. Preheat and Bake:
- Preheat your oven to 375°F (190°C).
- Bake the boule for 25-30 minutes or until the top is golden brown and the bread sounds hollow when tapped.

6. Cool and Enjoy:
- Allow the boule to cool in the pan for 10 minutes before transferring it to a wire rack to cool completely.

Nutrition Information (per serving):
(Note: Nutritional values are approximate and may vary based on specific ingredients used)
- Calories: 220
- Protein: 7g
- Carbohydrates: 35g
- Fat: 6g
- Saturated Fat: 2.5g
- Cholesterol: 15mg
- Fiber: 2g
- Sugars: 2g
- Sodium: 250mg

Embrace the culinary prowess of Gordon Ramsay as you indulge in the delightful experience of baking this Caramelized Onion and Gruyere Boule. A perfect addition to your repertoire of bread machine recipes, this savory creation is sure to be a hit at any gathering. Enjoy!

61. Lemon Herb Quinoa Bread

Elevate your bread machine repertoire with the zest and freshness of Lemon Herb Quinoa Bread—an inspired creation that combines the culinary prowess of Gordon Ramsay with the healthful goodness of quinoa. This delightful bread boasts a perfect balance of citrusy brightness and savory herbs, making it a unique and flavorful addition to your baking endeavors.

Serving: Makes one 2-pound loaf (approximately 12 slices).
Preparation Time: 15 minutes
Ready Time: 3 hours 30 minutes (including rising and baking time)

Ingredients:
- 1 cup cooked quinoa, cooled
- 1 cup warm water
- 2 tablespoons olive oil
- 1 tablespoon honey
- 1 lemon, zest and juice
- 3 cups bread flour
- 1 cup quinoa flour
- 1 teaspoon salt
- 2 teaspoons dried oregano
- 2 teaspoons dried thyme
- 2 teaspoons active dry yeast

Instructions:
1. In the bread machine pan, combine the warm water, olive oil, honey, and lemon juice and zest.
2. Add the bread flour, quinoa flour, salt, dried oregano, dried thyme, and cooked quinoa to the pan.
3. Make a small well in the dry ingredients and add the yeast.
4. Place the bread machine pan into the machine and select the "Basic" or "Whole Wheat" setting, depending on your machine's options. Choose the 2-pound loaf size and start the machine.
5. Allow the bread machine to complete its cycle, which typically includes mixing, kneading, rising, and baking.
6. Once the baking cycle is complete, carefully remove the bread from the machine and let it cool on a wire rack for at least 30 minutes before slicing.

Nutrition Information (per serving):
- Calories: 180
- Total Fat: 3g
- Saturated Fat: 0.5g
- Cholesterol: 0mg
- Sodium: 200mg
- Total Carbohydrates: 33g
- Dietary Fiber: 3g
- Sugars: 2g
- Protein: 6g

Note: Nutrition information is approximate and may vary based on specific ingredients and serving sizes.

Enjoy your Lemon Herb Quinoa Bread as a delightful accompaniment to soups, salads, or simply on its own for a burst of flavors!

62. Roasted Garlic Parmesan Knots

Elevate your bread machine game with these delectable Roasted Garlic Parmesan Knots inspired by the culinary genius, Gordon Ramsay. These irresistible knots are a perfect blend of savory roasted garlic and rich Parmesan cheese, creating a flavor profile that will leave your taste buds begging for more. Whether you're a seasoned chef or a home baker, this recipe promises to deliver a mouthwatering experience that will impress even the most discerning palates.

Serving: Makes approximately 12 knots
Preparation Time: 15 minutes
Ready Time: 2 hours (including rising and baking time)

Ingredients:
- 1 cup warm water (110°F/43°C)
- 2 tablespoons olive oil
- 1 teaspoon sugar
- 1 1/2 teaspoons salt
- 3 cups bread flour
- 2 1/4 teaspoons active dry yeast
- 1/4 cup unsalted butter, melted

- 3 cloves garlic, minced
- 1/2 cup grated Parmesan cheese
- 2 tablespoons fresh parsley, finely chopped
- Salt and black pepper, to taste

Instructions:
1. In the bread machine pan, combine warm water, olive oil, sugar, salt, bread flour, and active dry yeast. Select the dough cycle and start the machine. Allow the machine to knead and rise the dough.
2. Once the dough cycle is complete, transfer the dough to a floured surface. Preheat the oven to 375°F (190°C).
3. Roll the dough into a rectangle, approximately 12x18 inches.
4. In a small bowl, mix melted butter and minced garlic. Brush the garlic butter mixture evenly over the surface of the dough.
5. Sprinkle grated Parmesan cheese and chopped parsley evenly over the dough. Season with salt and black pepper to taste.
6. Cut the dough into 12 strips lengthwise. Tie each strip into a knot and place the knots on a parchment-lined baking sheet.
7. Bake in the preheated oven for 15-18 minutes or until the knots are golden brown.
8. Optional: Brush the knots with additional melted butter and sprinkle with extra Parmesan cheese and parsley before serving.

Nutrition Information:
Note: Nutritional values are approximate and may vary based on specific ingredients and serving sizes.
- Calories: 180 per knot
- Total Fat: 7g
- Saturated Fat: 3.5g
- Cholesterol: 15mg
- Sodium: 280mg
- Total Carbohydrates: 23g
- Dietary Fiber: 1g
- Sugars: 0.5g
- Protein: 5g

These Roasted Garlic Parmesan Knots are a delightful addition to any meal, or enjoy them on their own as a flavorful snack. Gordon Ramsay's influence shines through in this recipe, making it a must-try for bread enthusiasts and food lovers alike.

63. Sweet Potato Sage Dinner Rolls

Elevate your bread-making experience with these delectable Sweet Potato Sage Dinner Rolls, inspired by the culinary genius Gordon Ramsay. The combination of sweet potatoes and aromatic sage creates a unique flavor profile that will undoubtedly impress your taste buds. These rolls are perfect for any dinner table, adding a touch of warmth and sophistication to your meal.

Serving: Makes 12 dinner rolls.
Preparation Time: 15 minutes
Ready Time: 3 hours (including rising time)

Ingredients:
- 1 cup mashed sweet potatoes (about 2 medium-sized sweet potatoes, peeled, boiled, and mashed)
- 1/2 cup warm milk (110°F/43°C)
- 1/4 cup unsalted butter, melted
- 1/4 cup honey
- 1 large egg
- 1 teaspoon salt
- 1 tablespoon chopped fresh sage
- 4 cups all-purpose flour
- 2 1/4 teaspoons active dry yeast

Instructions:
1. Prepare Sweet Potatoes:
- Peel, dice, and boil the sweet potatoes until they are fork-tender. Mash them until smooth. Measure out 1 cup for the recipe.
2. Activate Yeast:
- In a bowl, combine warm milk and honey. Sprinkle the active dry yeast over the mixture and let it sit for 5-10 minutes until it becomes foamy.
3. Mix Wet Ingredients:
- In a large mixing bowl, combine the mashed sweet potatoes, melted butter, beaten egg, and chopped sage. Add the activated yeast mixture and mix well.
4. Add Dry Ingredients:

- Gradually add the flour and salt to the wet ingredients, stirring continuously until a soft dough forms.
5. Knead Dough:
- Turn the dough out onto a floured surface and knead for about 8-10 minutes, or until the dough is smooth and elastic.
6. First Rise:
- Place the dough in a lightly oiled bowl, cover it with a damp cloth, and let it rise in a warm place for about 1-1.5 hours, or until it has doubled in size.
7. Shape Rolls:
- Punch down the dough and divide it into 12 equal portions. Shape each portion into a ball and place them in a greased baking dish.
8. Second Rise:
- Cover the rolls with a damp cloth and let them rise for another 1-1.5 hours, or until they have doubled in size.
9. Bake:
- Preheat the oven to 375°F (190°C). Bake the rolls for 20-25 minutes, or until they are golden brown on top.
10. Serve:
- Allow the rolls to cool slightly before serving. Enjoy these Sweet Potato Sage Dinner Rolls with your favorite meals!

Nutrition Information:
- *Serving Size:* 1 roll
- *Calories:* 200
- *Total Fat:* 5g
- *Saturated Fat:* 3g
- *Cholesterol:* 25mg
- *Sodium:* 220mg
- *Total Carbohydrates:* 35g
- *Dietary Fiber:* 2g
- *Sugars:* 6g
- *Protein:* 4g

Note: Nutrition information is approximate and may vary based on specific ingredients used.

64. Raspberry Almond Bread

Indulge your taste buds with the delightful fusion of sweet and nutty flavors in this Raspberry Almond Bread recipe. Inspired by the culinary genius of Gordon Ramsay, this bread machine creation is a perfect balance of simplicity and sophistication. The vibrant burst of raspberries combined with the rich essence of almonds will elevate your bread experience to new heights. Prepare to embark on a journey of exquisite taste with every slice.

Serving: Makes one loaf (approximately 12 slices)
Preparation Time: 15 minutes
Ready Time: 3 hours (including rise and bake time)

Ingredients:
- 1 cup fresh raspberries
- 1/2 cup slivered almonds
- 1 cup warm water (110°F/43°C)
- 2 tablespoons olive oil
- 3 cups bread flour
- 1/4 cup granulated sugar
- 1 teaspoon salt
- 1 1/2 teaspoons active dry yeast

Instructions:
1. In the bread machine pan, combine warm water, olive oil, bread flour, sugar, and salt in the order recommended by the manufacturer.
2. Make a well in the center of the flour mixture and add the active dry yeast. Ensure that the yeast does not come into direct contact with the salt.
3. Place the bread machine pan in the machine and select the "Sweet Bread" or "Fruit and Nut" setting, if available. Alternatively, use the basic white bread setting.
4. Add the fresh raspberries and slivered almonds when the machine indicates it's time to add mix-ins or additional ingredients. This typically occurs during the kneading cycle.
5. Close the lid and let the bread machine complete the cycle. Once the baking process is complete, carefully remove the bread from the machine and allow it to cool on a wire rack.
6. Once cooled, slice the Raspberry Almond Bread and savor the delightful combination of flavors.

Nutrition Information:
(Per serving, based on 12 slices)
- Calories: 180
- Total Fat: 5g
- Saturated Fat: 0.5g
- Cholesterol: 0mg
- Sodium: 200mg
- Total Carbohydrates: 30g
- Dietary Fiber: 2g
- Sugars: 5g
- Protein: 5g

Note: Nutrition information is approximate and may vary based on specific ingredients used.

65. Asiago and Herb Sourdough

Elevate your bread machine experience with this delightful Asiago and Herb Sourdough recipe, inspired by the culinary genius of Gordon Ramsay. The rich flavors of Asiago cheese combined with the aromatic herbs create a heavenly fusion in each slice. With the convenience of your bread machine, you can effortlessly enjoy the artisanal taste of sourdough bread with a gourmet twist. Get ready to impress your taste buds and elevate your bread game!

Serving: Makes one delicious loaf, approximately 12 slices.
Preparation Time: 15 minutes
Ready Time: 3 hours and 30 minutes

Ingredients:
- 1 cup warm water (about 110°F/43°C)
- 2 tablespoons olive oil
- 1 1/2 teaspoons salt
- 1 tablespoon sugar
- 3 cups bread flour
- 1/2 cup grated Asiago cheese
- 2 teaspoons dried Italian herbs (basil, oregano, thyme)
- 1 1/2 teaspoons active dry yeast

Instructions:
1. Place the ingredients into your bread machine in the order recommended by the manufacturer.
2. Select the "Sourdough" setting on your machine. If your machine doesn't have a specific sourdough setting, choose the "White Bread" setting.
3. Start the machine, and let it work its magic! The dough will go through the kneading, rising, and baking phases.
4. About 10 minutes into the kneading phase, check the dough's consistency. It should form a smooth, elastic ball. If the dough is too sticky, add a little flour; if it's too dry, add a touch of water.
5. When the machine signals that the bread is ready, carefully remove the hot loaf. Allow it to cool on a wire rack for at least 30 minutes before slicing.

Nutrition Information:
(Per Slice, based on 12 slices)
- Calories: 180
- Total Fat: 4g
- Saturated Fat: 1.5g
- Trans Fat: 0g
- Cholesterol: 5mg
- Sodium: 350mg
- Total Carbohydrates: 30g
- Dietary Fiber: 1g
- Sugars: 1g
- Protein: 5g

Enjoy your freshly baked Asiago and Herb Sourdough, perfect for any meal or as a gourmet snack. This bread pairs wonderfully with soups, salads, or simply toasted with a pat of butter.

66. Pistachio Apricot Focaccia

Indulge your taste buds in a symphony of flavors with this delectable Pistachio Apricot Focaccia, a delightful creation inspired by the culinary genius of Gordon Ramsay. This unique bread machine recipe combines the rich, nutty notes of pistachios with the sweet and tangy essence of apricots, creating a perfect balance of savory and sweet. The golden, pillowy focaccia, adorned with vibrant apricot jewels and crunchy pistachio bits, is a feast for both the eyes and the palate. Elevate your bread-making experience with this Gordon Ramsay-inspired creation that brings together simplicity and sophistication in every bite.

Serving: Serve this Pistachio Apricot Focaccia as a delightful accompaniment to your favorite cheeses, or savor it on its own with a drizzle of honey. Ideal for brunches, afternoon teas, or as an elegant addition to any meal.
Preparation Time: 15 minutes
Ready Time: 2 hours (including rising time)

Ingredients:
- 1 cup warm water (110°F/43°C)
- 2 tablespoons olive oil
- 3 cups bread flour
- 1 teaspoon sugar
- 1 teaspoon salt
- 2 teaspoons active dry yeast
- 1/2 cup shelled pistachios, roughly chopped
- 1/2 cup dried apricots, chopped
- Extra olive oil for drizzling
- Sea salt for sprinkling

Instructions:
1. In the bread machine pan, combine warm water and olive oil.
2. Add the bread flour, sugar, and salt to the pan, making a well in the center. Place the active dry yeast in the well.
3. Select the "Dough" setting on your bread machine and start the cycle. Allow the machine to knead and rise the dough.
4. Once the dough cycle is complete, transfer the dough to a lightly floured surface. Gently knead in the chopped pistachios and dried apricots until evenly distributed.
5. Preheat your oven to 375°F (190°C). Place the dough on a parchment-lined baking sheet and shape it into a rectangle or oval.
6. Drizzle the surface of the dough with extra olive oil and sprinkle with sea salt.
7. Allow the focaccia to rise for an additional 30 minutes in a warm place.

8. Bake in the preheated oven for 20-25 minutes or until the focaccia is golden brown and sounds hollow when tapped on the bottom.
9. Cool on a wire rack before slicing.

Nutrition Information:
Note: Nutrition information may vary based on specific ingredients used and serving sizes.
Calories per serving: XXX
Total Fat: XXg
Saturated Fat: XXg
Cholesterol: XXmg
Sodium: XXXmg
Total Carbohydrates: XXg
Dietary Fiber: XXg
Sugars: XXg
Protein: XXg
Enjoy the culinary masterpiece that is the Pistachio Apricot Focaccia – a true testament to the art of bread making inspired by the renowned Gordon Ramsay.

67. Rosemary Sea Salt Bagels

Elevate your breakfast game with these Rosemary Sea Salt Bagels inspired by the culinary genius of Gordon Ramsay. The aromatic essence of rosemary combined with the subtle crunch of sea salt creates a bagel that's not only visually appealing but also bursting with flavor. Perfectly golden and delightfully chewy, these bagels are a testament to the artistry of bread-making in the comfort of your own home.

Serving: Makes 6 bagels
Preparation Time: 15 minutes
Ready Time: 3 hours

Ingredients:
- 1 1/2 cups warm water (110°F/43°C)
- 4 cups bread flour
- 2 tablespoons sugar
- 1 1/2 teaspoons salt

- 1 tablespoon dried rosemary, finely chopped
- 2 teaspoons active dry yeast
- 1 tablespoon olive oil
- 1 tablespoon honey
- Coarse sea salt, for topping

Instructions:
1. In the bread machine pan, combine warm water, bread flour, sugar, salt, dried rosemary, and active dry yeast in the order recommended by your bread machine manufacturer.
2. Select the dough cycle and start the machine. Allow it to knead and rise until the cycle is complete.
3. Once the dough has risen, preheat your oven to 425°F (220°C).
4. Turn the dough out onto a floured surface and divide it into 6 equal portions. Shape each portion into a smooth ball, then poke a hole in the center and gently stretch to form a bagel shape.
5. In a large pot, bring water to a boil. Add honey to the boiling water. Boil the bagels, two at a time, for 1-2 minutes on each side. Using a slotted spoon, transfer the boiled bagels to a parchment-lined baking sheet.
6. Brush the tops of the bagels with olive oil and sprinkle with coarse sea salt.
7. Bake in the preheated oven for 15-20 minutes or until the bagels are golden brown.
8. Allow the bagels to cool on a wire rack before slicing and serving.

Nutrition Information:
Per serving (1 bagel):
- Calories: 290
- Total Fat: 2g
- Saturated Fat: 0.3g
- Cholesterol: 0mg
- Sodium: 595mg
- Total Carbohydrates: 59g
- Dietary Fiber: 2g
- Sugars: 4g
- Protein: 8g

Enjoy these Rosemary Sea Salt Bagels warm from the oven with your favorite spread or toppings for a delightful breakfast or brunch experience.

68. Blue Cheese and Walnut Bread

Indulge your taste buds with a delectable twist on traditional bread machine recipes with this enticing Blue Cheese and Walnut Bread. Inspired by the culinary genius of Gordon Ramsay, this bread combines the rich and tangy flavor of blue cheese with the earthy crunch of walnuts, creating a delightful fusion of textures and tastes. Perfect for elevating your bread game to a whole new level, this recipe will become a staple in your kitchen.

Serving: Makes one loaf (approximately 12 slices)
Preparation Time: 15 minutes
Ready Time: 3 hours and 30 minutes

Ingredients:
- 1 cup warm water (110°F/43°C)
- 2 tablespoons olive oil
- 3 cups bread flour
- 1 teaspoon salt
- 2 tablespoons sugar
- 1 ½ teaspoons active dry yeast
- 1 cup crumbled blue cheese
- 1 cup chopped walnuts

Instructions:
1. Prepare the Bread Machine:
- Ensure your bread machine is clean and ready for use.
- Insert the kneading paddle into the bread pan.
2. Add Wet Ingredients:
- Pour the warm water and olive oil into the bread pan.
3. Add Dry Ingredients:
- In a separate bowl, whisk together the bread flour, salt, and sugar.
- Add the dry ingredients to the bread pan on top of the wet ingredients.
4. Create a Well for Yeast:
- Make a small well in the center of the flour mixture.
- Place the active dry yeast in the well.
5. Start the Bread Machine:

- Place the bread pan into the bread machine.
- Select the appropriate setting for basic white bread or a similar option on your machine.
- Start the machine.

6. Incorporate Blue Cheese and Walnuts:
- When the machine signals for additions (usually after the initial mixing phase), add the crumbled blue cheese and chopped walnuts.
- Allow the machine to continue its cycle.

7. Monitor the Dough:
- Keep an eye on the dough consistency during the kneading phase. If it appears too dry, add a tablespoon of water at a time until a soft, elastic dough forms.

8. Cool and Slice:
- Once the bread machine completes its cycle, carefully remove the hot loaf from the pan.
- Allow the bread to cool on a wire rack before slicing.

Nutrition Information:
- *Serving Size:* 1 slice (1/12 of the loaf)
- *Calories:* Approximately 220
- *Total Fat:* 12g
- *Saturated Fat:* 3g
- *Cholesterol:* 10mg
- *Sodium:* 280mg
- *Total Carbohydrates:* 22g
- *Dietary Fiber:* 2g
- *Sugars:* 2g
- *Protein:* 7g

Elevate your bread experience with this Blue Cheese and Walnut Bread, a culinary masterpiece that perfectly balances savory and nutty notes. Inspired by Gordon Ramsay's ingenuity, this recipe is sure to become a favorite in your kitchen, impressing family and friends alike. Enjoy it as a standalone snack, with soups, or as a gourmet addition to your cheese platter.

69. Pumpkin Seed Spelt Bread

Elevate your bread machine game with this Pumpkin Seed Spelt Bread, inspired by the culinary genius of Gordon Ramsay. This hearty and nutritious loaf combines the nutty flavors of spelt flour with the earthiness of pumpkin seeds, resulting in a bread that's not only delicious but also packed with wholesome goodness. Let your bread machine do the work while you enjoy the delightful aroma of freshly baked bread wafting through your kitchen.

Serving: Makes one 2-pound loaf, approximately 16 slices.
Preparation Time: 15 minutes
Ready Time: 3 hours 45 minutes

Ingredients:
- 1 1/2 cups warm water (about 110°F/43°C)
- 2 tablespoons olive oil
- 2 tablespoons honey
- 3 1/2 cups spelt flour
- 1 1/2 cups all-purpose flour
- 1 1/2 teaspoons salt
- 2 teaspoons active dry yeast
- 1/2 cup pumpkin seeds (plus extra for topping)

Instructions:
1. Preparation:
- Place the warm water, olive oil, and honey in the bread machine pan.
2. Dry Ingredients:
- In a separate bowl, combine the spelt flour, all-purpose flour, and salt.
3. Layering:
- Add the flour mixture on top of the wet ingredients in the bread machine pan.
4. Yeast:
- Make a small well in the center of the flour mixture and add the yeast.
5. Kneading:
- Set your bread machine to the "Dough" cycle and start the process. Allow the machine to knead the ingredients together, forming a smooth and elastic dough.
6. Pumpkin Seeds:
- When the machine signals, add the pumpkin seeds. Let the machine continue until the dough has completed its cycle.
7. Shaping:

- Remove the dough from the machine and place it on a floured surface. Shape it into a round loaf.
8. Second Rise:
- Transfer the shaped dough to a greased and floured bread pan. Cover with a clean kitchen towel and let it rise in a warm place for about 1 hour, or until it doubles in size.
9. Preheat:
- Preheat your oven to 375°F (190°C).
10. Topping:
- Sprinkle additional pumpkin seeds over the top of the risen loaf.
11. Baking:
- Bake in the preheated oven for 30-35 minutes or until the bread is golden brown and sounds hollow when tapped on the bottom.
12. Cooling:
- Allow the bread to cool in the pan for 10 minutes, then transfer it to a wire rack to cool completely.

Nutrition Information (per slice):
- Calories: 150
- Total Fat: 4g
- Saturated Fat: 0.5g
- Cholesterol: 0mg
- Sodium: 180mg
- Total Carbohydrates: 26g
- Dietary Fiber: 4g
- Sugars: 2g
- Protein: 5g

Enjoy this Pumpkin Seed Spelt Bread as a delightful accompaniment to your meals or toasted with your favorite spread!

70. Orange Cranberry Pistachio Bread

Elevate your bread-making game with this delightful Orange Cranberry Pistachio Bread, inspired by the culinary genius of Gordon Ramsay. The combination of zesty orange, tart cranberries, and crunchy pistachios creates a flavor symphony that will leave your taste buds singing. Perfectly crafted for your bread machine, this recipe guarantees a deliciously moist and aromatic loaf every time.

Serving: Yields one 2-pound loaf, approximately 12 slices.
Preparation Time: 15 minutes
Ready Time: 3 hours (may vary based on bread machine settings)

Ingredients:
- 1 cup warm water
- 1/4 cup orange juice
- 2 tablespoons orange zest
- 3 tablespoons unsalted butter, softened
- 3 cups bread flour
- 1/4 cup sugar
- 1 teaspoon salt
- 1 1/2 teaspoons active dry yeast
- 1/2 cup dried cranberries
- 1/2 cup shelled pistachios, coarsely chopped

Instructions:
1. Prepare the Bread Machine:
- Ensure your bread machine is clean and in good working condition.
- Place the warm water, orange juice, orange zest, and softened butter into the bread pan.
2. Add Dry Ingredients:
- In a separate bowl, whisk together the bread flour, sugar, and salt.
- Pour the dry ingredients on top of the wet ingredients in the bread pan.
3. Create a Well for Yeast:
- Make a small well in the center of the flour mixture and add the active dry yeast.
4. Load the Cranberries and Pistachios:
- Sprinkle the dried cranberries and chopped pistachios evenly over the top of the flour mixture.
5. Insert Bread Pan:
- Place the bread pan into the bread machine, ensuring it's securely in place.
6. Select Settings:
- Choose the appropriate settings on your bread machine for a 2-pound loaf, sweet bread, and light crust.
7. Start the Machine:
- Press the start button to begin the bread-making process. Allow the machine to mix, knead, rise, and bake the bread.

8. Cool and Slice:
- Once the bread machine signals completion, carefully remove the pan and let the bread cool on a wire rack for at least 15 minutes before slicing.

9. Serve and Enjoy:
- Serve slices of Orange Cranberry Pistachio Bread on their own or toasted with a pat of butter. The burst of citrus, complemented by the tartness of cranberries and the crunch of pistachios, makes for a delightful treat.

Nutrition Information:
- *Serving Size:* 1 slice (1/12 of loaf)
- *Calories:* Approximately 180
- *Total Fat:* 5g
- *Saturated Fat:* 2g
- *Cholesterol:* 8mg
- *Sodium:* 200mg
- *Total Carbohydrates:* 31g
- *Dietary Fiber:* 2g
- *Sugars:* 7g
- *Protein:* 5g

Enjoy this Orange Cranberry Pistachio Bread as a delightful addition to your breakfast or as a tasty snack any time of the day. Inspired by the culinary prowess of Gordon Ramsay, it's a bread machine recipe that combines simplicity with gourmet flavors.

71. Sage and Brown Butter Pretzel Buns

Elevate your bread machine game with these Sage and Brown Butter Pretzel Buns, inspired by the culinary genius of Gordon Ramsay. The aromatic blend of sage and the rich nuttiness of brown butter come together to create a flavor profile that's both sophisticated and comforting. These buns are perfect for sandwiches, sliders, or simply enjoyed on their own. Let your bread machine do the work as you savor the delicious results.

Serving: Makes 12 pretzel buns.
Preparation Time: 15 minutes

Ready Time: 2 hours (including rise time)

Ingredients:
- 1 cup warm milk (110°F/43°C)
- 2 1/4 teaspoons active dry yeast
- 1/4 cup brown sugar
- 1/4 cup unsalted butter, melted
- 3 1/2 cups all-purpose flour
- 1 teaspoon salt
- 2 tablespoons chopped fresh sage
- 1/4 cup baking soda
- 1 large egg, beaten (for egg wash)
- Coarse salt, for sprinkling

Instructions:
1. In the bread machine pan, combine the warm milk, active dry yeast, and brown sugar. Let it sit for 5 minutes until it becomes frothy.
2. Add the melted butter, all-purpose flour, salt, and chopped sage to the bread machine pan.
3. Set the bread machine to the dough setting and let it run its cycle.
4. Preheat your oven to 425°F (220°C).
5. Once the dough is ready, turn it out onto a floured surface. Divide it into 12 equal portions and shape them into balls.
6. In a large pot, bring water to a boil. Add the baking soda and reduce to a simmer. Carefully drop each dough ball into the simmering water for about 30 seconds. Remove with a slotted spoon and place them on a parchment-lined baking sheet.
7. Brush each bun with the beaten egg and sprinkle with coarse salt.
8. Bake in the preheated oven for 12-15 minutes or until the buns are golden brown.
9. Allow the buns to cool slightly before serving.

Nutrition Information:
Per serving (1 bun):
- Calories: 210
- Total Fat: 6g
- Saturated Fat: 3.5g
- Cholesterol: 30mg
- Sodium: 400mg
- Total Carbohydrates: 33g

- Dietary Fiber: 1g
- Sugars: 4g
- Protein: 6g

Enjoy these Sage and Brown Butter Pretzel Buns warm from the oven, and savor the delightful combination of flavors with every bite. Perfect for any occasion, these buns are a testament to the artistry of bread making, with a touch of Gordon Ramsay-inspired culinary finesse.

72. Cheddar Bacon Jalapeño Cornbread

Elevate your bread machine game with this delectable Cheddar Bacon Jalapeño Cornbread recipe, inspired by the culinary genius of Gordon Ramsay. The combination of sharp cheddar, smoky bacon, and a hint of jalapeño creates a flavor explosion that will leave your taste buds tingling. Whether served as a side dish or enjoyed on its own, this cornbread is a savory delight that's easy to prepare in your trusty bread machine.

Serving: Makes 12 slices
Preparation Time: 15 minutes
Ready Time: 2 hours and 30 minutes

Ingredients:
- 1 cup cornmeal
- 1 cup all-purpose flour
- 1 tablespoon baking powder
- 1/2 teaspoon baking soda
- 1/2 teaspoon salt
- 1 cup buttermilk
- 2 large eggs
- 1/4 cup unsalted butter, melted
- 1 cup sharp cheddar cheese, shredded
- 1/2 cup cooked bacon, crumbled
- 1-2 jalapeños, seeds removed and finely chopped

Instructions:
1. Preparation: Grease the bread machine pan lightly.
2. Dry Ingredients: In a mixing bowl, combine the cornmeal, all-purpose flour, baking powder, baking soda, and salt.

3. Wet Ingredients: In a separate bowl, whisk together the buttermilk and eggs. Add the melted butter and mix well.
4. Combine: Pour the wet ingredients into the bread machine pan, followed by the dry ingredients. Set the machine to the "Quick Bread" or "Cornbread" setting.
5. Add Flavors: During the last few minutes of the mixing cycle, add the shredded cheddar, crumbled bacon, and chopped jalapeños. Allow the machine to finish the mixing and baking process.
6. Check for Doneness: Insert a toothpick into the center; if it comes out clean, the cornbread is done.
7. Cool and Serve: Let the cornbread cool in the pan for 10 minutes before transferring it to a wire rack. Slice and serve warm.

Nutrition Information (per serving):
- Calories: 210
- Total Fat: 10g
- Saturated Fat: 6g
- Cholesterol: 55mg
- Sodium: 400mg
- Total Carbohydrates: 22g
- Dietary Fiber: 2g
- Sugars: 1g
- Protein: 7g

Enjoy the rich flavors of Cheddar Bacon Jalapeño Cornbread, a mouthwatering creation that perfectly blends the expertise of Gordon Ramsay with the convenience of your bread machine.

73. Fig and Walnut Artisan Loaf

Elevate your bread machine baking skills with this exquisite Fig and Walnut Artisan Loaf, a creation inspired by the culinary genius of Gordon Ramsay. The combination of sweet figs and crunchy walnuts in a rustic artisanal bread will transport your taste buds to a new level of delight. This recipe not only captures the essence of artisanal craftsmanship but also brings a touch of sophistication to your table.

Serving: Makes one 1.5-pound loaf, approximately 12 slices.
Preparation Time: 15 minutes

Ready Time: 3 hours (including rise and bake time)

Ingredients:
- 1 cup warm water (110°F/43°C)
- 2 tablespoons olive oil
- 1 teaspoon honey
- 1 1/2 teaspoons salt
- 3 cups bread flour
- 1 teaspoon active dry yeast
- 1/2 cup dried figs, chopped
- 1/2 cup walnuts, chopped

Instructions:
1. Prepare the Bread Machine:
Place the warm water, olive oil, honey, and salt into the bread machine pan.
2. Add the Dry Ingredients:
Measure and add the bread flour to the pan. Create a small well in the center of the flour and place the active dry yeast in the well.
3. Set the Bread Machine:
Select the appropriate setting for a 1.5-pound loaf and choose the medium crust setting. Start the bread machine.
4. Incorporate Figs and Walnuts:
Once the machine signals to add extra ingredients (usually during the kneading cycle), add the chopped figs and walnuts. Allow the machine to continue its cycle.
5. Monitor the Dough:
Keep an eye on the dough during the initial mixing and kneading phase. If it appears too sticky, add a tablespoon of flour at a time until a smooth, elastic dough forms.
6. Shape the Loaf:
Once the machine completes the dough cycle, remove the dough and shape it into a round or oval loaf. Place it on a parchment-lined baking sheet.
7. Final Rise:
Cover the shaped dough with a clean kitchen towel and let it rise in a warm place for about 1-2 hours or until doubled in size.
8. Preheat and Bake:

Preheat your oven to 375°F (190°C). Bake the risen loaf for 25-30 minutes or until golden brown. You can tap the bottom; it should sound hollow when it's done.

9. Cool and Slice:

Allow the Fig and Walnut Artisan Loaf to cool on a wire rack before slicing.

Nutrition Information (per serving):
Note: Nutritional values are approximate and may vary based on specific ingredients and serving sizes.
- Calories: 180
- Total Fat: 7g
- Saturated Fat: 1g
- Trans Fat: 0g
- Cholesterol: 0mg
- Sodium: 290mg
- Total Carbohydrates: 26g
- Dietary Fiber: 2g
- Sugars: 4g
- Protein: 5g

Enjoy this delightful Fig and Walnut Artisan Loaf as a standalone treat or paired with your favorite cheeses and spreads. Elevate your bread machine expertise with the touch of Gordon Ramsay-inspired culinary flair!

74. Cinnamon Raisin Walnut Challah

Indulge your senses in the delightful symphony of flavors with this Cinnamon Raisin Walnut Challah recipe, a creation inspired by the culinary genius of Gordon Ramsay. This bread machine masterpiece combines the richness of cinnamon, the sweetness of raisins, and the crunch of walnuts, resulting in a heavenly loaf that's perfect for any occasion. Whether you're a novice or an experienced baker, this recipe promises a delectable outcome that will impress even the most discerning palates.

Serving: Makes one large loaf
Preparation Time: 15 minutes

Ready Time: 3 hours (including rising and baking time)

Ingredients:
- 1 cup warm water (110°F/43°C)
- 3 tablespoons vegetable oil
- 1/4 cup honey
- 2 large eggs
- 4 cups bread flour
- 1 teaspoon salt
- 1 tablespoon ground cinnamon
- 1/2 cup raisins
- 1/2 cup chopped walnuts
- 2 1/4 teaspoons active dry yeast

Instructions:
1. Prepare the Bread Machine:
Place the warm water, vegetable oil, honey, and eggs into the bread machine pan.
2. Add Dry Ingredients:
In a separate bowl, whisk together the bread flour, salt, and ground cinnamon. Add this mixture on top of the wet ingredients in the bread machine pan.
3. Create a Well:
Make a well in the center of the flour mixture and add the raisins and chopped walnuts into the well.
4. Add Yeast:
Make a small indentation in the dry ingredients and add the active dry yeast.
5. Start the Machine:
Place the bread machine pan into the machine and select the "Dough" setting. Press start and let the machine work its magic, allowing the dough to mix and rise.
6. Shape the Challah:
Once the dough cycle is complete, turn the dough out onto a floured surface. Divide the dough into three equal portions and roll each portion into a long rope. Braid the ropes together and place the braided loaf on a parchment-lined baking sheet.
7. Second Rise:
Cover the braided challah with a clean kitchen towel and let it rise for an additional 30-45 minutes or until it doubles in size.

8. Preheat and Bake:
Preheat the oven to 350°F (175°C). Bake the challah for 25-30 minutes or until it's golden brown and sounds hollow when tapped on the bottom.

9. Cool and Enjoy:
Allow the challah to cool on a wire rack before slicing. Serve slices on their own or with a dollop of honey butter for an extra touch of indulgence.

Nutrition Information:
Note: Nutrition information is approximate and may vary based on specific ingredients used.
- Calories per serving: XXX
- Total Fat: XXg
- Cholesterol: XXmg
- Sodium: XXXmg
- Total Carbohydrates: XXg
- Dietary Fiber: XXg
- Sugars: XXg
- Protein: XXg

Prepare to savor every bite of this Cinnamon Raisin Walnut Challah, a bread machine creation that seamlessly blends simplicity with sophistication. Inspired by the renowned Gordon Ramsay, this recipe guarantees a loaf that's both visually stunning and irresistibly delicious.

75. Garlic Parmesan Pizza Dough

Elevate your pizza experience with this Garlic Parmesan Pizza Dough, inspired by the culinary genius of Gordon Ramsay. The aromatic blend of garlic and the rich flavor of Parmesan cheese take this classic dough to new heights, creating a perfect canvas for your favorite pizza toppings.

Serving: 4 servings
Preparation Time: 15 minutes
Ready Time: 1 hour 30 minutes

Ingredients:
- 1 cup warm water (110°F/43°C)

- 1 tablespoon sugar
- 2 1/4 teaspoons active dry yeast
- 2 1/2 cups all-purpose flour
- 1 teaspoon salt
- 3 tablespoons olive oil
- 2 cloves garlic, minced
- 1/2 cup grated Parmesan cheese
- 1 teaspoon dried oregano
- Cornmeal (for dusting)

Instructions:
1. In a small bowl, combine warm water and sugar. Stir until the sugar dissolves. Sprinkle the active dry yeast over the water and let it sit for about 5 minutes, or until it becomes foamy.
2. In the bowl of your bread machine, add the flour and salt. Pour in the yeast mixture and olive oil.
3. Set your bread machine to the "Dough" setting and let it run until a smooth and elastic dough forms, usually for about 10 minutes.
4. While the dough is kneading, mix minced garlic, Parmesan cheese, and dried oregano in a small bowl.
5. Once the dough is ready, transfer it to a lightly floured surface and roll it out into your desired pizza shape.
6. Preheat your oven to 450°F (230°C).
7. Sprinkle cornmeal on a pizza stone or baking sheet. Place the rolled-out dough on the stone or sheet.
8. Evenly spread the garlic Parmesan mixture over the dough, leaving a small border around the edges for the crust.
9. Bake in the preheated oven for 12-15 minutes or until the crust is golden and the cheese is melted and bubbly.
10. Remove from the oven, let it cool for a few minutes, slice, and serve.

Nutrition Information (per serving):
- Calories: 320
- Fat: 10g
- Saturated Fat: 3g
- Cholesterol: 5mg
- Sodium: 550mg
- Carbohydrates: 48g
- Fiber: 2g
- Sugar: 1g

- Protein: 9g

Note: Nutrition information is approximate and may vary based on specific ingredients used.

76. Smoked Salmon and Dill Focaccia

Elevate your bread machine game with this delectable recipe inspired by the culinary genius, Gordon Ramsay. The Smoked Salmon and Dill Focaccia is a sophisticated twist on a classic Italian bread, combining the richness of smoked salmon with the freshness of dill. Perfect for brunches, lunches, or as an elegant appetizer, this bread machine creation will leave your taste buds tingling with delight.

Serving: 8 slices
Preparation Time: 15 minutes
Ready Time: 2 hours and 30 minutes (including baking and resting)

Ingredients:
- 1 cup warm water (110°F/43°C)
- 2 tablespoons olive oil
- 1 teaspoon sugar
- 1 teaspoon salt
- 3 cups bread flour
- 1 1/2 teaspoons active dry yeast
- 100g smoked salmon, thinly sliced
- 2 tablespoons fresh dill, chopped
- 1 tablespoon capers (optional)
- 1 tablespoon lemon zest
- 1 tablespoon olive oil (for drizzling)
- Sea salt, for sprinkling

Instructions:
1. Place the warm water, olive oil, sugar, and salt in the bread machine pan.
2. Add the bread flour on top of the liquid ingredients, creating a mound in the center. Make a well in the center of the flour and add the yeast.
3. Set the bread machine to the "dough" cycle and start the process. Allow the machine to knead and rise the dough.

4. Once the dough cycle is complete, remove the dough from the machine and roll it out onto a floured surface, forming a rectangle.
5. Transfer the dough to a parchment-lined baking sheet. Cover it with a clean kitchen towel and let it rise for 30-45 minutes, or until it doubles in size.
6. Preheat your oven to 375°F (190°C).
7. Once the dough has risen, use your fingertips to make dimples in the dough's surface. Drizzle the dough with olive oil and sprinkle with sea salt.
8. Bake in the preheated oven for 20-25 minutes or until the focaccia is golden brown and sounds hollow when tapped on the bottom.
9. Allow the focaccia to cool for a few minutes before topping it with smoked salmon, fresh dill, capers (if using), and lemon zest.
10. Slice the focaccia into 8 pieces and serve warm.

Nutrition Information (per serving):
- Calories: 220
- Total Fat: 8g
- Saturated Fat: 1g
- Cholesterol: 5mg
- Sodium: 380mg
- Total Carbohydrates: 29g
- Dietary Fiber: 1g
- Sugars: 0g
- Protein: 9g

Indulge in the luxurious flavors of this Smoked Salmon and Dill Focaccia, a masterpiece inspired by the culinary expertise of Gordon Ramsay. Whether you're hosting a gathering or simply craving a gourmet treat, this bread machine recipe is sure to impress.

77. Pesto Sunflower Seed Bread

Elevate your bread machine game with this delightful Pesto Sunflower Seed Bread inspired by the culinary genius, Gordon Ramsay. The aromatic blend of fresh basil pesto and the nutty crunch of sunflower seeds will transport your taste buds to a whole new level of delight. Perfect for sandwiches, toast, or enjoyed on its own, this bread is a testament to the harmony of flavors in every bite.

Serving: 8-10 slices
Preparation Time: 15 minutes
Ready Time: 3 hours (including rise and bake time)

Ingredients:
- 1 cup warm water (110°F/43°C)
- 2 tablespoons olive oil
- 3 cups bread flour
- 1/4 cup sunflower seeds
- 1/4 cup basil pesto
- 1 tablespoon sugar
- 1 teaspoon salt
- 2 1/4 teaspoons active dry yeast

Instructions:
1. Prepare the Bread Machine:
- Ensure your bread machine is clean and ready for use.
2. Add Wet Ingredients:
- Pour the warm water and olive oil into the bread machine pan.
3. Add Dry Ingredients:
- In a separate bowl, combine the bread flour, sunflower seeds, sugar, and salt.
- Add the dry ingredients to the bread machine pan.
4. Create a Well:
- Make a well in the center of the dry ingredients and add the active dry yeast.
5. Pesto Infusion:
- Spoon the basil pesto into the well with the yeast, ensuring it does not directly touch the liquid.
6. Start the Machine:
- Place the bread machine pan into the bread machine.
- Set the machine to the "Basic" or "White Bread" setting, medium crust.
- Start the machine, allowing it to complete the full cycle.
7. Cooling:
- Once the baking cycle is complete, carefully remove the bread pan from the machine.
- Allow the bread to cool in the pan for 10 minutes before transferring it to a wire rack to cool completely.
8. Slice and Serve:

- Once the Pesto Sunflower Seed Bread has cooled, slice it into 8-10 pieces.
- Serve it as a delightful accompaniment to your favorite dishes or enjoy it on its own.

Nutrition Information:
- *Note: Nutritional values may vary depending on specific ingredients and serving sizes.*
- Serving Size: 1 slice
- Calories: 180
- Total Fat: 7g
- Saturated Fat: 1g
- Trans Fat: 0g
- Cholesterol: 0mg
- Sodium: 250mg
- Total Carbohydrates: 26g
- Dietary Fiber: 2g
- Sugars: 1g
- Protein: 5g

Elevate your bread machine experience with this Pesto Sunflower Seed Bread, a fusion of Gordon Ramsay's inspiration and your culinary mastery. Enjoy the delightful aroma and taste of homemade goodness with every slice.

78. Cranberry Orange Walnut Sourdough

Elevate your bread machine game with this Cranberry Orange Walnut Sourdough inspired by the culinary genius, Gordon Ramsay. Bursting with the tangy goodness of cranberries, the citrusy zing of oranges, and the nutty crunch of walnuts, this sourdough bread is a delightful twist on a classic. Ramsay's influence shines through in the harmonious blend of flavors and the artisanal touch that sets this bread apart.

Serving: Makes one loaf, approximately 12 slices.
Preparation Time: 15 minutes
Ready Time: 3 hours, 30 minutes (including rise and bake time)

Ingredients:

- 1 cup active sourdough starter
- 1 1/2 cups bread flour
- 1 1/2 cups whole wheat flour
- 1 cup dried cranberries
- 1/2 cup chopped walnuts
- Zest of one orange
- 1 tablespoon orange juice
- 1 1/2 teaspoons salt
- 1 cup lukewarm water

Instructions:
1. In the bread machine pan, combine the active sourdough starter, bread flour, whole wheat flour, dried cranberries, chopped walnuts, orange zest, and salt.
2. Pour in the lukewarm water and orange juice.
3. Place the bread machine pan into the bread machine and set it to the "Dough" cycle. Allow the machine to knead and rise the dough.
4. Once the dough cycle is complete, remove the dough from the machine and place it on a floured surface. Shape it into a round loaf.
5. Preheat your oven to 375°F (190°C).
6. Transfer the shaped dough to a parchment-lined baking sheet or a cast-iron Dutch oven.
7. Score the top of the dough with a sharp knife in a decorative pattern.
8. Bake in the preheated oven for 30-35 minutes or until the bread is golden brown and sounds hollow when tapped on the bottom.
9. Allow the bread to cool on a wire rack before slicing.

Nutrition Information:
(Per serving - 1 slice)
- Calories: 150
- Total Fat: 4g
- Saturated Fat: 0.5g
- Cholesterol: 0mg
- Sodium: 200mg
- Total Carbohydrates: 26g
- Dietary Fiber: 3g
- Sugars: 6g
- Protein: 4g

Note: Nutrition information is approximate and may vary based on specific ingredients and serving sizes.

79. Chive and Gouda Beer Bread

Elevate your bread machine experience with this delectable Chive and Gouda Beer Bread inspired by the culinary genius of Gordon Ramsay. This savory loaf boasts the robust flavors of chives and the rich creaminess of Gouda cheese, all brought together with the distinct touch of beer. Perfect for any occasion, this bread will impress your guests and tantalize your taste buds.

Serving: Makes one 1.5-pound loaf (approximately 12 slices)
Preparation Time: 15 minutes
Ready Time: 3 hours (including baking time)

Ingredients:
- 1 cup beer (preferably a light ale or lager)
- 3 cups bread flour
- 1 cup shredded Gouda cheese
- 1/4 cup chopped fresh chives
- 2 tablespoons sugar
- 1 teaspoon salt
- 1 1/2 teaspoons active dry yeast

Instructions:
1. Begin by ensuring that all ingredients are at room temperature for optimal results.
2. In the bread machine pan, pour the beer.
3. Add the bread flour, shredded Gouda cheese, chopped chives, sugar, and salt on top of the beer.
4. Make a small well in the center of the dry ingredients and add the active dry yeast.
5. Place the bread machine pan into the bread machine and select the "Basic" or "White Bread" setting. Choose the desired crust color and loaf size (1.5 pounds).
6. Start the bread machine and let it work its magic. The machine will mix, knead, rise, and bake the bread.
7. Once the baking cycle is complete, carefully remove the hot bread pan from the machine.

8. Allow the bread to cool in the pan for 10 minutes, then transfer it to a wire rack to cool completely before slicing.

Nutrition Information:
Note: Nutritional values are approximate and may vary based on specific ingredients used.
- Serving Size: 1 slice
- Calories: 150
- Total Fat: 4g
- Saturated Fat: 2.5g
- Cholesterol: 15mg
- Sodium: 200mg
- Total Carbohydrates: 22g
- Dietary Fiber: 1g
- Sugars: 1g
- Protein: 6g

Whether enjoyed on its own, toasted with butter, or as a side to your favorite soup, this Chive and Gouda Beer Bread is a delightful addition to your bread machine repertoire. Get ready to savor the delicious fusion of flavors in every bite!

80. Sundried Tomato Basil Baguette

Elevate your bread machine experience with this delectable Sundried Tomato Basil Baguette inspired by the culinary genius of Gordon Ramsay. Bursting with vibrant flavors and aromatic herbs, this bread is a delightful addition to any meal or can be enjoyed on its own. The simplicity of a bread machine meets the sophistication of Gordon Ramsay's taste in this easy-to-follow recipe.

Serving: Makes one flavorful baguette, approximately 12 slices.
Preparation Time: 15 minutes
Ready Time: 3 hours (including rising and baking time)

Ingredients:
- 1 cup warm water
- 2 tablespoons olive oil
- 1 teaspoon sugar

- 1 1/2 teaspoons salt
- 3 cups bread flour
- 2 teaspoons active dry yeast
- 1/3 cup sundried tomatoes, finely chopped
- 2 tablespoons fresh basil, chopped
- 1 teaspoon garlic powder
- Extra flour for dusting

Instructions:
1. In the bread machine pan, combine warm water, olive oil, sugar, and salt.
2. Add the bread flour, creating a well in the center, and place the yeast in the well.
3. Select the dough cycle on your bread machine and start the process.
4. Once the dough has completed its cycle, transfer it to a floured surface and gently knead in the sundried tomatoes, fresh basil, and garlic powder until evenly distributed.
5. Shape the dough into a baguette and place it on a parchment-lined baking sheet. Cover with a clean kitchen towel and let it rise in a warm place for about 1 hour or until doubled in size.
6. Preheat the oven to 375°F (190°C).
7. Make shallow diagonal slashes across the top of the baguette with a sharp knife.
8. Bake for 25-30 minutes or until the bread is golden brown and sounds hollow when tapped.
9. Allow the baguette to cool on a wire rack before slicing.

Nutrition Information:
(Per serving - 1 slice)
- Calories: 120
- Total Fat: 3g
- Saturated Fat: 0.5g
- Cholesterol: 0mg
- Sodium: 290mg
- Total Carbohydrates: 20g
- Dietary Fiber: 1g
- Sugars: 1g
- Protein: 4g

Indulge in the rich flavors of sundried tomatoes and basil with every bite of this artisanal baguette—a true testament to the perfect union of simplicity and sophistication in the world of bread-making.

81. Caramelized Onion and Thyme Brioche

Elevate your bread machine game with the delectable combination of sweet caramelized onions and fragrant thyme in this Caramelized Onion and Thyme Brioche. Inspired by the culinary genius of Gordon Ramsay, this recipe takes the simplicity of a bread machine and transforms it into a gourmet delight. The rich, buttery brioche paired with the savory-sweet profile of caramelized onions and the earthy notes of thyme create a bread that's perfect for any occasion.

Serving: Makes one loaf (approximately 12 slices)
Preparation Time: 20 minutes
Ready Time: 3 hours (including rising and baking time)

Ingredients:
- 1 cup caramelized onions (about 2 large onions, thinly sliced)
- 3 tablespoons fresh thyme leaves, chopped
- 1 cup whole milk, warmed
- 3 large eggs
- 1/2 cup unsalted butter, softened
- 4 cups bread flour
- 1/4 cup granulated sugar
- 1 1/2 teaspoons salt
- 2 1/4 teaspoons active dry yeast

Instructions:
1. In the bread machine pan, combine the warm milk, eggs, and softened butter.
2. Add the bread flour on top, creating a mound, and make a small well in the center. Place the sugar, salt, and yeast in the well.
3. Set the bread machine to the "dough" cycle and let it run. This will mix and knead the ingredients, allowing the dough to rise.

4. Once the dough cycle is complete, transfer the dough to a floured surface. Gently fold in the caramelized onions and thyme until evenly distributed.

5. Shape the dough into a loaf and place it in a greased loaf pan. Cover with a clean kitchen towel and let it rise in a warm place for about 1-2 hours or until doubled in size.

6. Preheat the oven to 350°F (175°C). Bake the brioche for 30-35 minutes or until golden brown on top and sounds hollow when tapped.

7. Allow the brioche to cool in the pan for 10 minutes before transferring it to a wire rack to cool completely.

Nutrition Information:
(Per Serving - 1 slice)
- Calories: 240
- Total Fat: 8g
- Saturated Fat: 4.5g
- Cholesterol: 60mg
- Sodium: 230mg
- Total Carbohydrates: 34g
- Dietary Fiber: 2g
- Sugars: 4g
- Protein: 7g

Enjoy this Caramelized Onion and Thyme Brioche on its own, toasted, or as a side to your favorite dishes. Your bread machine has never produced something so sophisticated and flavorful!

82. Walnut Rosemary Olive Bread

Elevate your bread-making experience with this delightful Walnut Rosemary Olive Bread, inspired by the culinary genius of Gordon Ramsay. Infused with the aromatic essence of rosemary, the rich crunch of walnuts, and the savory burst of olives, this bread is a symphony of flavors that will impress even the most discerning palates. Let your bread machine do the work, while you savor the anticipation of a fragrant and artisanal loaf that's perfect for any occasion.

Serving: This Walnut Rosemary Olive Bread serves 8-10 people.
Preparation Time: 15 minutes

Ready Time: 3 hours

Ingredients:
- 1 cup warm water (110°F/43°C)
- 2 tablespoons olive oil
- 3 cups bread flour
- 1 teaspoon sugar
- 1 teaspoon salt
- 1 1/2 teaspoons active dry yeast
- 1/2 cup chopped walnuts
- 1/3 cup pitted and chopped Kalamata olives
- 2 tablespoons fresh rosemary, finely chopped

Instructions:
1. Place the warm water, olive oil, bread flour, sugar, salt, and active dry yeast into the bread machine pan, following the manufacturer's instructions for the order.
2. Select the "Dough" cycle on your bread machine and start the process. Allow the machine to knead and rise the dough.
3. Once the dough cycle is complete, remove the dough from the machine and place it on a lightly floured surface.
4. Flatten the dough and evenly distribute the chopped walnuts, olives, and rosemary over the surface.
5. Fold the dough over the added ingredients and knead for a few minutes until they are well incorporated.
6. Shape the dough into a round or oval loaf and place it in a greased and floured bread pan.
7. Cover the pan with a clean kitchen towel and let the dough rise in a warm place for about 1-1.5 hours or until it has doubled in size.
8. Preheat the oven to 375°F (190°C).
9. Bake the bread for 25-30 minutes or until it is golden brown on top and sounds hollow when tapped.
10. Allow the bread to cool in the pan for 10 minutes before transferring it to a wire rack to cool completely.

Nutrition Information:
Note: Nutrition information is per serving (1 slice, based on 10 servings)
- Calories: 220
- Total Fat: 9g

- Saturated Fat: 1g
- Trans Fat: 0g
- Cholesterol: 0mg
- Sodium: 300mg
- Total Carbohydrates: 28g
- Dietary Fiber: 2g
- Sugars: 0.5g
- Protein: 6g

Indulge in the irresistible combination of textures and flavors with this Walnut Rosemary Olive Bread – a creation that embodies the essence of Gordon Ramsay's culinary mastery.

83. Roasted Red Pepper and Feta Bread

Indulge your senses in the irresistible symphony of flavors with our Roasted Red Pepper and Feta Bread—a culinary masterpiece inspired by the renowned Gordon Ramsay. This bread is a celebration of the harmonious marriage between the smoky sweetness of roasted red peppers and the rich tanginess of feta cheese. Each bite is a journey through the artisanal expertise of Gordon Ramsay, bringing you a loaf that is not just bread but a work of art.

Serving: Makes one loaf, approximately 12 slices.
Preparation Time: 15 minutes
Ready Time: 3 hours (includes rising and baking time)

Ingredients:
- 1 cup roasted red peppers, diced
- 1 cup crumbled feta cheese
- 3 1/2 cups bread flour
- 1 1/2 teaspoons salt
- 1 tablespoon sugar
- 1 1/2 teaspoons active dry yeast
- 1 cup warm water
- 2 tablespoons olive oil

Instructions:
1. *Prepare the Bread Machine:*

Ensure your bread machine is clean and functioning correctly. Insert the kneading paddle into the machine pan.
2. *Combine Wet Ingredients:*
In a bowl, mix warm water and active dry yeast. Allow it to sit for 5 minutes until it becomes frothy. Add olive oil to the yeast mixture.
3. *Combine Dry Ingredients:*
In a separate bowl, whisk together bread flour, salt, and sugar.
4. *Load the Bread Machine:*
Place the wet ingredients into the bread machine pan. Add the dry ingredients on top. Make a well in the center of the flour mixture and add the roasted red peppers and feta cheese.
5. *Start the Machine:*
Insert the bread machine pan into the bread maker. Select the appropriate setting for basic or white bread and start the machine.
6. *Monitor the Dough:*
Keep an eye on the dough during the initial mixing phase. If it appears too dry, add a tablespoon of water at a time. If it's too sticky, add a tablespoon of flour at a time.
7. *Wait Patiently:*
Allow the bread machine to complete the full cycle, including the rising and baking phases.
8. *Cool and Slice:*
Once the baking is complete, carefully remove the hot bread from the machine. Allow it to cool on a wire rack before slicing.

Nutrition Information:
(Per Slice, assuming 12 slices)
- Calories: 180
- Total Fat: 6g
- Saturated Fat: 3g
- Trans Fat: 0g
- Cholesterol: 15mg
- Sodium: 300mg
- Total Carbohydrates: 25g
- Dietary Fiber: 1g
- Sugars: 1g
- Protein: 6g

Elevate your bread-making skills with this Gordon Ramsay-inspired Roasted Red Pepper and Feta Bread—a perfect blend of culinary expertise and delectable flavors.

84. Pumpkin Sage Fougasse

Elevate your bread machine experience with this Pumpkin Sage Fougasse, a delightful creation inspired by the culinary genius of Gordon Ramsay. The subtle sweetness of pumpkin combined with the earthy aroma of sage creates a unique and irresistible flavor profile. Perfect for impressing your guests or indulging in a cozy homemade treat.

Serving: 1 Fougasse
Preparation Time: 15 minutes
Ready Time: 3 hours (including rising and baking)

Ingredients:
- 1 cup canned pumpkin puree
- 1/4 cup olive oil
- 1 tablespoon honey
- 1 tablespoon active dry yeast
- 3 1/2 cups bread flour
- 1 teaspoon salt
- 1 tablespoon finely chopped fresh sage
- Olive oil (for brushing)
- Coarse sea salt (for sprinkling)

Instructions:
1. In a small bowl, combine the active dry yeast with 1/4 cup warm water and let it sit for 5 minutes, or until it becomes frothy.
2. In the bread machine pan, combine the pumpkin puree, olive oil, honey, flour, salt, and the yeast mixture. Select the dough setting and start the machine.
3. When the dough cycle is complete, preheat your oven to 400°F (200°C).
4. Remove the dough from the machine and place it on a floured surface. Punch it down and knead in the chopped sage until evenly distributed.
5. Roll out the dough into an oval shape, about 1/2-inch thick. With a sharp knife, make diagonal cuts on each side of the oval, leaving a thicker strip in the center to resemble a leaf.

6. Gently stretch and pull the dough to widen the cuts, creating a leaf-like shape. Transfer the fougasse to a parchment-lined baking sheet.
7. Brush the surface of the fougasse with olive oil and sprinkle with coarse sea salt.
8. Bake in the preheated oven for 20-25 minutes or until golden brown and crusty.
9. Allow the Pumpkin Sage Fougasse to cool for a few minutes before slicing and serving.

Nutrition Information:
Note: Nutritional values are approximate and may vary based on specific ingredients used.
- Calories: 200 per serving
- Total Fat: 7g
- Saturated Fat: 1g
- Trans Fat: 0g
- Cholesterol: 0mg
- Sodium: 300mg
- Total Carbohydrates: 30g
- Dietary Fiber: 2g
- Sugars: 3g
- Protein: 5g

Enjoy the delightful flavors of this Pumpkin Sage Fougasse – a masterpiece inspired by the culinary expertise of Gordon Ramsay. Perfectly baked in your bread machine, it's a treat for your senses and a star at any dining table.

85. Lemon Blueberry Almond Loaf

Indulge your taste buds in a symphony of flavors with our delectable Lemon Blueberry Almond Loaf inspired by the culinary genius of Gordon Ramsay. This delightful bread machine recipe combines the zesty brightness of lemons, the burst of sweet blueberries, and the nutty richness of almonds to create a moist and flavorful loaf that's perfect for any occasion.

Serving: 8-10 slices
Preparation Time: 15 minutes

Ready Time: 3 hours (including baking time)

Ingredients:
- 1 cup fresh blueberries
- 2 tablespoons lemon zest
- 1/2 cup sliced almonds
- 3 cups all-purpose flour
- 1 packet (2 1/4 teaspoons) active dry yeast
- 1/4 cup granulated sugar
- 1 teaspoon salt
- 1 cup warm milk
- 1/4 cup unsalted butter, melted
- 2 large eggs
- 1 teaspoon almond extract
- Cooking spray or extra butter for greasing

Instructions:
1. In a small bowl, combine the warm milk and active dry yeast. Let it sit for 5 minutes until the yeast is activated and becomes frothy.
2. In the bowl of your bread machine, add the activated yeast mixture, all-purpose flour, sugar, salt, melted butter, eggs, and almond extract.
3. Set the bread machine to the "dough" setting and let it run through the kneading and rising cycles.
4. Once the dough cycle is complete, gently fold in the fresh blueberries, lemon zest, and sliced almonds until evenly distributed.
5. Grease a loaf pan with cooking spray or butter.
6. Transfer the dough into the prepared loaf pan, spreading it evenly.
7. Cover the loaf pan with a clean kitchen towel and let the dough rise for an additional 45-60 minutes, or until it has doubled in size.
8. Preheat your oven to 350°F (175°C).
9. Bake the loaf in the preheated oven for 30-40 minutes, or until the top is golden brown and a toothpick inserted into the center comes out clean.
10. Allow the Lemon Blueberry Almond Loaf to cool in the pan for 10 minutes before transferring it to a wire rack to cool completely.

Nutrition Information:
(Per slice, based on 10 slices)
- Calories: 250
- Total Fat: 8g

- Saturated Fat: 3.5g
- Cholesterol: 45mg
- Sodium: 230mg
- Total Carbohydrates: 38g
- Dietary Fiber: 2g
- Sugars: 8g
- Protein: 6g

Indulge in the delightful fusion of citrusy goodness, juicy blueberries, and crunchy almonds with every bite of this Lemon Blueberry Almond Loaf. Perfect for breakfast, brunch, or a sweet treat anytime!

86. Cheddar Jalapeño Pretzel Rolls

Indulge your taste buds in a culinary journey inspired by the renowned Gordon Ramsay with these delectable Cheddar Jalapeño Pretzel Rolls. A perfect blend of bold flavors, these rolls bring together the richness of cheddar cheese and the fiery kick of jalapeños, all wrapped in the comforting warmth of a soft pretzel exterior. Elevate your bread machine skills and impress your guests with this irresistible twist on a classic favorite.

Serving: Makes 12 rolls
Preparation Time: 15 minutes
Ready Time: 2 hours, 30 minutes (including rise time)

Ingredients:
- 1 cup warm water (110°F/43°C)
- 1 tablespoon sugar
- 2 1/4 teaspoons active dry yeast
- 3 cups all-purpose flour
- 1 teaspoon salt
- 1 cup shredded sharp cheddar cheese
- 1/4 cup finely chopped pickled jalapeños
- 1/4 cup baking soda
- 1 large egg, beaten (for egg wash)
- Coarse sea salt, for sprinkling

Instructions:

1. In the bread machine pan, combine warm water and sugar. Sprinkle the yeast over the top and let it sit for 5 minutes, or until foamy.
2. Add the flour, salt, cheddar cheese, and chopped jalapeños to the bread machine pan.
3. Select the dough cycle and start the machine. Allow it to knead and rise until the cycle is complete.
4. Preheat the oven to 425°F (220°C). Line a baking sheet with parchment paper.
5. Punch down the risen dough and turn it out onto a lightly floured surface. Divide it into 12 equal portions and shape each into a ball.
6. In a large pot, bring water to a boil. Add the baking soda.
7. Boil each dough ball in the baking soda water for 30 seconds, then transfer to the prepared baking sheet.
8. Brush each roll with the beaten egg and sprinkle with coarse sea salt.
9. Bake for 12-15 minutes or until the rolls are golden brown.
10. Allow the Cheddar Jalapeño Pretzel Rolls to cool slightly before serving.

Nutrition Information:
(Per Serving)
- Calories: 220
- Total Fat: 5g
- Saturated Fat: 3g
- Cholesterol: 25mg
- Sodium: 580mg
- Total Carbohydrates: 35g
- Dietary Fiber: 2g
- Sugars: 1g
- Protein: 9g

Enjoy these Cheddar Jalapeño Pretzel Rolls warm from the oven, and savor the combination of gooey cheddar and spicy jalapeños in every delightful bite. Inspired by the culinary genius of Gordon Ramsay, this recipe is a testament to the artistry of bread-making in your very own kitchen.

87. Honey Wheat Sunflower Seed Bread

Elevate your bread machine game with this Honey Wheat Sunflower Seed Bread recipe, inspired by the culinary prowess of Gordon Ramsay. This delightful loaf combines the wholesome goodness of whole wheat with the sweet richness of honey and the nutty crunch of sunflower seeds. The result is a bread that's not only delicious but also a testament to the artistry of home baking. Let the aroma of freshly baked bread fill your kitchen as you embark on a culinary journey guided by one of the world's most celebrated chefs.

Serving: Yields one 2-pound loaf, approximately 16 slices.
Preparation Time: 15 minutes
Ready Time: 3 hours (including rising and baking time)

Ingredients:
- 1 1/2 cups warm water (110°F/43°C)
- 3 tablespoons honey
- 2 tablespoons olive oil
- 2 cups whole wheat flour
- 1 1/2 cups bread flour
- 1 1/2 teaspoons salt
- 2 teaspoons active dry yeast
- 1/2 cup sunflower seeds, toasted

Instructions:
1. Place the warm water, honey, and olive oil in the bread machine pan.
2. In a separate bowl, combine the whole wheat flour, bread flour, and salt.
3. Add the flour mixture to the bread machine pan on top of the liquid ingredients.
4. Make a small well in the center of the flour and add the yeast.
5. Set the bread machine to the whole wheat setting and a 2-pound loaf size. Start the machine.
6. When the machine signals, add the toasted sunflower seeds.
7. Allow the bread machine to complete the cycle, including the rising and baking phases.
8. Once the baking is complete, carefully remove the bread from the pan and let it cool on a wire rack before slicing.

Nutrition Information:
Per Serving (1 slice):

- Calories: 150
- Total Fat: 4g
- Saturated Fat: 0.5g
- Trans Fat: 0g
- Cholesterol: 0mg
- Sodium: 200mg
- Total Carbohydrates: 26g
- Dietary Fiber: 3g
- Sugars: 4g
- Protein: 4g

Note: Nutrition values are approximate and may vary based on specific ingredients used.

88. Prosciutto and Fig Baguette

Elevate your bread machine experience with the exquisite flavors of this Prosciutto and Fig Baguette, inspired by the culinary genius of Gordon Ramsay. The combination of savory prosciutto, sweet figs, and crusty baguette creates a delightful symphony of tastes that will transport your taste buds to a gourmet paradise.

Serving: Serves 4
Preparation Time: 15 minutes
Ready Time: 2 hours and 30 minutes (including bread machine cycle)

Ingredients:
- 1 cup warm water
- 2 tablespoons olive oil
- 3 cups bread flour
- 1 teaspoon sugar
- 1 teaspoon salt
- 1 1/2 teaspoons active dry yeast
- 6-8 slices prosciutto
- 8-10 fresh figs, sliced
- 1/2 cup crumbled goat cheese
- 2 tablespoons honey
- Fresh thyme leaves for garnish

Instructions:
1. Place the warm water, olive oil, bread flour, sugar, salt, and active dry yeast into the bread machine pan in the order recommended by the manufacturer.
2. Select the dough setting on your bread machine and start the cycle. Allow the machine to knead and rise the dough.
3. Once the dough cycle is complete, transfer the dough to a lightly floured surface. Roll it out into a rectangle.
4. Preheat your oven to 375°F (190°C).
5. Layer the prosciutto, sliced figs, and crumbled goat cheese evenly over the dough.
6. Starting from one of the longer edges, roll the dough tightly into a log. Pinch the seam to seal.
7. Place the rolled dough on a baking sheet lined with parchment paper. Make a few diagonal slashes on the top with a sharp knife.
8. Allow the dough to rise for an additional 30 minutes.
9. Bake in the preheated oven for 25-30 minutes or until the baguette is golden brown.
10. Drizzle honey over the top of the baked baguette and sprinkle with fresh thyme leaves.
11. Allow the baguette to cool for a few minutes before slicing.

Nutrition Information:
Note: Nutritional values are approximate and may vary based on specific ingredients used and portion sizes.
- Calories per serving: 350
- Total Fat: 12g
- Saturated Fat: 4g
- Trans Fat: 0g
- Cholesterol: 20mg
- Sodium: 500mg
- Total Carbohydrates: 50g
- Dietary Fiber: 4g
- Sugars: 12g
- Protein: 12g

Indulge in the sophistication of this Prosciutto and Fig Baguette, a delightful creation that effortlessly blends the richness of prosciutto with the sweetness of figs, all encased in a perfect, homemade baguette. This recipe, inspired by Gordon Ramsay, is sure to impress both friends and family alike.

89. Parmesan Garlic Herb Ciabatta

Elevate your bread machine experience with this delectable Parmesan Garlic Herb Ciabatta inspired by the culinary genius, Gordon Ramsay. The perfect combination of savory Parmesan, aromatic garlic, and fragrant herbs makes this ciabatta a standout in the realm of homemade bread. Impress your taste buds and guests with the irresistible flavors and golden crust of this artisanal delight.

Serving: Makes 1 loaf (approximately 12 slices)
Preparation Time: 15 minutes
Ready Time: 3 hours (including rise and bake time)

Ingredients:
- 1 cup warm water (about 110°F/43°C)
- 2 tablespoons olive oil
- 3 cups bread flour
- 1 teaspoon sugar
- 1 1/2 teaspoons salt
- 1 tablespoon dried oregano
- 1 tablespoon dried basil
- 1 tablespoon dried parsley
- 2 teaspoons garlic powder
- 2 teaspoons active dry yeast
- 1 cup grated Parmesan cheese

Instructions:
1. Preparation:
- Ensure your bread machine is clean and ready for use.
- In a small bowl, combine warm water and sugar. Sprinkle the yeast over the water and let it sit for 5 minutes until it becomes frothy.
2. Dry Ingredients:
- In the bread machine pan, combine bread flour, salt, dried oregano, dried basil, dried parsley, and garlic powder.
3. Wet Ingredients:
- Pour the activated yeast mixture and olive oil into the bread machine pan with the dry ingredients.

4. Kneading and Rising:
- Select the dough setting on your bread machine and let it run its course. This typically includes kneading and the first rise. Allow the machine to complete the cycle.

5. Shaping:
- Once the dough cycle is complete, transfer the dough onto a floured surface. Shape it into a rectangle and sprinkle half of the grated Parmesan cheese over the surface. Fold the dough in half and sprinkle the remaining Parmesan on top. Fold the dough again, incorporating the cheese.

6. Final Rise:
- Place the shaped dough on a parchment-lined baking sheet. Cover it with a clean kitchen towel and let it rise for an additional 30-45 minutes, or until doubled in size.

7. Baking:
- Preheat the oven to 375°F (190°C). Bake the ciabatta for 20-25 minutes or until golden brown and sounds hollow when tapped.

8. Cooling:
- Allow the Parmesan Garlic Herb Ciabatta to cool on a wire rack before slicing.

Nutrition Information:
(Per serving - 1 slice)
- Calories: 160
- Total Fat: 5g
- Saturated Fat: 2g
- Cholesterol: 8mg
- Sodium: 290mg
- Total Carbohydrates: 23g
- Dietary Fiber: 1g
- Sugars: 1g
- Protein: 6g

Enjoy this artisanal delight as a side to your favorite pasta dish or on its own with a dab of butter. A slice of heaven awaits in every bite!

90. Apricot Almond Rye Bread

Indulge your taste buds in the delightful symphony of flavors with our Apricot Almond Rye Bread. Inspired by the culinary genius of Gordon Ramsay, this bread machine recipe combines the earthy richness of rye, the natural sweetness of apricots, and the nutty crunch of almonds. Perfect for breakfast or as an accompaniment to your favorite dishes, this bread is a testament to the art of artisanal baking made easy in your own kitchen.

Serving: Makes one loaf, approximately 12 slices.
Preparation Time: 15 minutes
Ready Time: 3 hours

Ingredients:
- 1 cup warm water
- 2 tablespoons olive oil
- 3 tablespoons honey
- 1 cup whole wheat flour
- 1 1/2 cups rye flour
- 1 cup bread flour
- 1 teaspoon salt
- 1 1/2 teaspoons active dry yeast
- 1/2 cup dried apricots, finely chopped
- 1/3 cup sliced almonds

Instructions:
1. Place the warm water, olive oil, and honey in the bread machine pan.
2. In a separate bowl, mix the whole wheat flour, rye flour, bread flour, and salt together.
3. Add the flour mixture to the bread machine pan.
4. Make a small well in the center of the flour and add the active dry yeast.
5. Start the bread machine on the dough setting, allowing it to mix and knead the ingredients. This process usually takes about 10-15 minutes.
6. Once the dough has formed, add the chopped apricots and sliced almonds. Allow the machine to continue kneading until the ingredients are evenly distributed.
7. Stop the machine and let the dough rise in the pan for about 1.5 to 2 hours or until it has doubled in size.
8. Preheat your oven to 350°F (175°C).

9. Remove the dough from the machine and shape it into a loaf. Place the loaf in a greased bread pan.

10. Bake for 25-30 minutes or until the bread is golden brown and sounds hollow when tapped.

11. Allow the bread to cool in the pan for 10 minutes, then transfer it to a wire rack to cool completely before slicing.

Nutrition Information:
Note: Nutrition information is approximate and may vary based on specific ingredients used and serving sizes.
- Serving Size: 1 slice
- Calories: 150
- Total Fat: 4g
- Saturated Fat: 0.5g
- Cholesterol: 0mg
- Sodium: 200mg
- Total Carbohydrates: 25g
- Dietary Fiber: 3g
- Sugars: 6g
- Protein: 4g

Enjoy the rustic charm and wholesome goodness of this Apricot Almond Rye Bread—a creation that embodies the essence of Gordon Ramsay's culinary inspiration.

91. Basil Pesto Parmesan Fougasse

Elevate your bread machine game with this delectable Basil Pesto Parmesan Fougasse recipe, inspired by the culinary genius of Gordon Ramsay. The aromatic blend of fresh basil, rich Parmesan, and a hint of pesto creates a flavorful masterpiece that will leave your taste buds dancing. This artisanal bread is not only a feast for the senses but also a testament to the magic that happens when quality ingredients meet the convenience of modern technology.

Serving: Makes one large Fougasse, serving 8-10.
Preparation Time: 15 minutes
Ready Time: 2 hours 30 minutes (includes rising time)

Ingredients:
- 1 cup warm water
- 2 tablespoons olive oil
- 1 teaspoon sugar
- 1 1/2 teaspoons salt
- 3 cups bread flour
- 2 teaspoons active dry yeast
- 1/2 cup fresh basil leaves, finely chopped
- 1/4 cup Parmesan cheese, grated
- 2 tablespoons pesto sauce

Instructions:
1. In the bread machine pan, combine warm water, olive oil, sugar, and salt.
2. Add the bread flour to the pan, creating a mound in the center. Make a well in the center of the flour and add the yeast.
3. Place the pan in the bread machine, select the dough cycle, and start the machine.
4. While the dough is mixing, prepare a baking sheet by lining it with parchment paper.
5. Once the dough cycle is complete, transfer the dough onto a floured surface. Gently knead in the chopped basil, Parmesan cheese, and pesto until well incorporated.
6. Roll out the dough into a rectangle and transfer it to the prepared baking sheet.
7. Using a sharp knife or pizza cutter, make diagonal cuts on both sides of the dough, leaving a wide strip down the center.
8. Carefully lift every other strip and twist it to the side, repeating until the strips form a braided pattern.
9. Cover the fougasse with a clean kitchen towel and let it rise for an additional 30-45 minutes.
10. Preheat your oven to 375°F (190°C).
11. Bake the fougasse in the preheated oven for 20-25 minutes or until golden brown.
12. Allow the bread to cool slightly before slicing and serving.

Nutrition Information:
(Per Serving - Based on 10 servings)
- Calories: 200
- Total Fat: 6g

- Saturated Fat: 1.5g
- Cholesterol: 3mg
- Sodium: 400mg
- Total Carbohydrates: 30g
- Dietary Fiber: 2g
- Sugars: 1g
- Protein: 6g

Indulge in the irresistible flavors of this Basil Pesto Parmesan Fougasse, a delightful creation that seamlessly merges the convenience of your bread machine with the culinary finesse inspired by Gordon Ramsay.

92. Dark Chocolate Cherry Challah

Indulge your senses in the exquisite blend of rich dark chocolate and succulent cherries with this heavenly Dark Chocolate Cherry Challah. Inspired by the culinary prowess of Gordon Ramsay, this bread machine recipe elevates the traditional challah to new heights. The combination of velvety dark chocolate and sweet cherries creates a delightful twist on a classic favorite. Perfect for any occasion, this bread is sure to become a staple in your home.

Serving: Makes one loaf, approximately 12 slices.
Preparation Time: 15 minutes
Ready Time: 3 hours (including rising and baking time)

Ingredients:
- 1 cup warm water
- 2 large eggs
- 1/4 cup vegetable oil
- 1/4 cup honey
- 1 teaspoon vanilla extract
- 4 cups bread flour
- 1 teaspoon salt
- 2 teaspoons active dry yeast
- 1 cup dark chocolate chips
- 1 cup dried cherries, chopped

Instructions:

1. Place the warm water, eggs, vegetable oil, honey, and vanilla extract into the bread machine pan in the order recommended by the manufacturer.
2. In a separate bowl, whisk together the bread flour and salt. Add this dry mixture on top of the wet ingredients in the bread machine.
3. Make a small well in the center of the flour and add the active dry yeast.
4. Set the bread machine to the dough setting and start the cycle. Allow the machine to knead and rise the dough.
5. Once the dough cycle is complete, remove the dough and place it on a floured surface. Gently flatten the dough and evenly sprinkle dark chocolate chips and chopped dried cherries over the surface.
6. Roll the dough into a log shape, ensuring that the chocolate chips and cherries are distributed evenly throughout.
7. Place the rolled dough into a greased loaf pan, cover with a kitchen towel, and let it rise for an additional 45 minutes.
8. Preheat the oven to 350°F (175°C).
9. Bake the challah in the preheated oven for 25-30 minutes or until the top is golden brown and the bread sounds hollow when tapped.
10. Allow the Dark Chocolate Cherry Challah to cool in the pan for 10 minutes before transferring it to a wire rack to cool completely.

Nutrition Information:
(Per serving - 1 slice)
- Calories: 280
- Total Fat: 9g
- Saturated Fat: 3g
- Cholesterol: 30mg
- Sodium: 180mg
- Total Carbohydrates: 45g
- Dietary Fiber: 2g
- Sugars: 14g
- Protein: 6g

Enjoy this Dark Chocolate Cherry Challah as a decadent treat, whether toasted with a pat of butter or savored on its own. Let the enticing aroma fill your kitchen and captivate your taste buds with every delightful bite.

93. Sun-dried Tomato Basil Sourdough

Elevate your bread machine game with this delightful Sun-dried Tomato Basil Sourdough recipe, inspired by the culinary genius of Gordon Ramsay. The combination of tangy sourdough, sun-dried tomatoes, and aromatic basil creates a loaf that's bursting with flavor. Enjoy the rustic charm and gourmet taste of this homemade bread that's perfect for any occasion.

Serving: Makes one loaf (approximately 10 slices)
Preparation Time: 15 minutes
Ready Time: 4 hours (including rising and baking time)

Ingredients:
- 1 cup active sourdough starter
- 1 1/2 cups warm water
- 4 cups bread flour
- 1/2 cup whole wheat flour
- 1/2 cup sun-dried tomatoes, chopped
- 1/4 cup fresh basil, finely chopped
- 1 1/2 teaspoons salt

Instructions:
1. In the bread machine pan, combine the active sourdough starter and warm water.
2. Add the bread flour, whole wheat flour, sun-dried tomatoes, fresh basil, and salt to the pan.
3. Place the pan into the bread machine, select the "dough" cycle, and press start. Allow the machine to mix and knead the ingredients until a smooth and elastic dough forms.
4. Once the dough cycle is complete, transfer the dough to a floured surface and shape it into a round loaf. Place the dough into a well-floured proofing basket or bowl, cover with a clean kitchen towel, and let it rise for about 2 hours or until doubled in size.
5. Preheat your oven to 450°F (230°C) and place a Dutch oven with the lid on in the oven to heat.
6. Once the dough has risen, carefully transfer it to the hot Dutch oven. Score the top of the dough with a sharp knife to allow for expansion.

7. Cover the Dutch oven with the lid and bake for 30 minutes. Then, remove the lid and bake for an additional 15 minutes or until the bread has a golden brown crust.
8. Allow the bread to cool on a wire rack before slicing.

Nutrition Information:
(Per Serving)
- Calories: 180
- Total Fat: 1g
- Saturated Fat: 0.2g
- Cholesterol: 0mg
- Sodium: 350mg
- Total Carbohydrates: 37g
- Dietary Fiber: 2.5g
- Sugars: 0.5g
- Protein: 6g

Indulge in the irresistible aroma and taste of this Sun-dried Tomato Basil Sourdough, a testament to the artistry of bread-making inspired by the renowned Gordon Ramsay.

94. Garlic Parmesan Rosemary Rolls

Elevate your bread machine skills with these delectable Garlic Parmesan Rosemary Rolls inspired by the culinary genius, Gordon Ramsay. Infused with the rich flavors of garlic, the nuttiness of Parmesan, and the aromatic essence of rosemary, these rolls are a perfect blend of sophistication and comfort. Let your bread machine do the hard work, while you enjoy the heavenly aroma and taste of these divine creations.

Serving: Makes 12 rolls
Preparation Time: 15 minutes
Ready Time: 2 hours (including rising and baking)

Ingredients:
- 1 cup warm milk (110°F/43°C)
- 2 tablespoons unsalted butter, melted
- 3 cloves garlic, minced
- 1 tablespoon fresh rosemary, finely chopped

- 3 cups all-purpose flour
- 1/4 cup grated Parmesan cheese
- 2 tablespoons sugar
- 1 teaspoon salt
- 2 1/4 teaspoons active dry yeast

Instructions:
1. Preparation:
- Ensure the bread machine is clean and ready for use.
- Mince the garlic and chop the fresh rosemary finely.
- Measure and prepare all other ingredients.
2. Loading the Bread Machine:
- In the bread machine pan, add the warm milk and melted butter.
- Sprinkle the minced garlic and chopped rosemary over the liquids.
- Add the all-purpose flour, Parmesan cheese, sugar, and salt.
- Make a small well in the dry ingredients and add the active dry yeast.
3. Setting the Bread Machine:
- Place the bread machine pan into the machine and select the dough setting.
- Start the machine, allowing it to knead and rise the dough.
4. Shaping the Rolls:
- Once the dough cycle is complete, turn the dough out onto a floured surface.
- Divide the dough into 12 equal portions and shape each into a ball.
5. Second Rise:
- Place the shaped rolls on a greased baking sheet, leaving some space between them.
- Cover with a clean kitchen towel and let them rise for about 30-45 minutes, or until doubled in size.
6. Baking:
- Preheat the oven to 375°F (190°C).
- Bake the risen rolls in the preheated oven for 15-20 minutes or until golden brown.
- While baking, melt an additional tablespoon of butter and brush the tops of the rolls for a golden finish.
7. Cooling:
- Allow the rolls to cool on a wire rack for a few minutes before serving.

Nutrition Information (per roll):
- Calories: 180

- Total Fat: 5g
- Saturated Fat: 3g
- Cholesterol: 15mg
- Sodium: 220mg
- Total Carbohydrates: 28g
- Dietary Fiber: 1g
- Sugars: 1g
- Protein: 5g

Indulge in the irresistible combination of garlic, Parmesan, and rosemary with these exquisite rolls. Perfect for any occasion, these aromatic creations will leave your kitchen filled with the inviting fragrance of a bakery, impressing family and friends with every bite.

95. Fig and Goat Cheese Focaccia

Indulge your taste buds in a symphony of flavors with this Fig and Goat Cheese Focaccia, a delightful creation inspired by the culinary genius of Gordon Ramsay. This bread machine recipe combines the earthy sweetness of figs with the rich creaminess of goat cheese, elevating the classic focaccia to new heights. With a golden, crisp crust and a moist, airy interior, this bread is perfect for sharing at gatherings or savoring as a special treat.

Serving: Makes 1 large focaccia, approximately 12 slices.
Preparation Time: 15 minutes
Ready Time: 3 hours (including rising and baking time)

Ingredients:
- 1 cup warm water
- 2 tablespoons olive oil
- 3 cups bread flour
- 1 teaspoon sugar
- 1 teaspoon salt
- 1 packet (2 1/4 teaspoons) active dry yeast
- 1/2 cup goat cheese, crumbled
- 1/2 cup dried figs, sliced
- 2 tablespoons fresh rosemary, chopped
- Extra olive oil for drizzling

- Coarse sea salt for sprinkling

Instructions:
1. Prepare the Bread Machine:
- Place the warm water, olive oil, bread flour, sugar, salt, and active dry yeast in the bread machine in the order recommended by the manufacturer.
2. Select the Dough Setting:
- Set the bread machine to the dough setting and start the cycle. Allow the machine to knead and rise the dough.
3. Preheat the Oven:
- Preheat your oven to 400°F (200°C) and line a baking sheet with parchment paper.
4. Shape the Focaccia:
- Once the dough cycle is complete, transfer the dough to a floured surface. Roll or press the dough into a rectangle and place it on the prepared baking sheet.
5. Add Toppings:
- Spread the crumbled goat cheese evenly over the dough, followed by the sliced dried figs. Sprinkle with chopped fresh rosemary. Drizzle extra olive oil over the top and sprinkle with coarse sea salt.
6. Allow Final Rise:
- Let the topped dough rest and rise for about 20-30 minutes, or until it puffs up slightly.
7. Bake:
- Bake in the preheated oven for 20-25 minutes or until the focaccia is golden brown and cooked through.
8. Cool and Slice:
- Allow the Fig and Goat Cheese Focaccia to cool on a wire rack before slicing into squares or wedges.

Nutrition Information:
- *Note: Nutrition information is per serving (1 slice, assuming 12 slices)*
- Calories: XXX
- Total Fat: XXg
- Saturated Fat: XXg
- Cholesterol: XXmg
- Sodium: XXXmg
- Total Carbohydrates: XXg

- Dietary Fiber: XXg
- Sugars: XXg
- Protein: XXg

Enjoy the delightful blend of sweet figs and creamy goat cheese in every bite of this Fig and Goat Cheese Focaccia, a creation that seamlessly marries simplicity with sophistication. Inspired by the culinary prowess of Gordon Ramsay, this bread machine recipe is a testament to the artistry of home baking.

96. Cranberry Orange Cinnamon Bread

Elevate your bread machine baking skills with this delectable Cranberry Orange Cinnamon Bread inspired by the culinary genius of Gordon Ramsay. Bursting with the vibrant flavors of tart cranberries, zesty orange, and warm cinnamon, this bread is a delightful treat for any occasion. The ease of the bread machine ensures a hassle-free baking experience, allowing you to enjoy the rich aroma and taste of freshly baked bread without the fuss.

Serving: Makes one 2-pound loaf
Preparation Time: 15 minutes
Ready Time: 3 hours (including baking time)

Ingredients:
- 1 cup cranberries, fresh or frozen (thawed)
- Zest of 1 orange
- 1 cup orange juice
- 3 tablespoons unsalted butter, softened
- 3 cups bread flour
- 1/4 cup sugar
- 1 teaspoon salt
- 1 teaspoon ground cinnamon
- 1 1/2 teaspoons active dry yeast

Instructions:
1. Prepare the Ingredients:
- If using frozen cranberries, make sure to thaw them.
- Zest the orange, ensuring to avoid the bitter white pith.

2. Load the Bread Machine:
- In the bread machine pan, combine the cranberries, orange zest, orange juice, softened butter, bread flour, sugar, salt, cinnamon, and active dry yeast in the order recommended by your bread machine manufacturer.

3. Select the Dough Setting:
- Choose the appropriate setting on your bread machine for a 2-pound loaf and select the dough cycle.

4. Monitor the Dough:
- Keep an eye on the dough as it mixes and rises. Add a bit more flour or water if needed to achieve a smooth, elastic consistency.

5. Shape the Loaf:
- Once the dough cycle is complete, remove the dough from the machine and place it on a floured surface. Shape it into a loaf and transfer it to a greased 9x5-inch loaf pan.

6. Final Rise:
- Allow the shaped dough to rise in a warm place for about 30-45 minutes, or until it doubles in size.

7. Preheat and Bake:
- Preheat your oven to 350°F (175°C). Bake the bread for 25-30 minutes or until the top is golden brown and the loaf sounds hollow when tapped.

8. Cool and Enjoy:
- Allow the Cranberry Orange Cinnamon Bread to cool in the pan for 10 minutes before transferring it to a wire rack to cool completely.

Nutrition Information:
- (Per serving - based on 16 slices)
- Calories: 160
- Total Fat: 3.5g
- Saturated Fat: 2g
- Cholesterol: 8mg
- Sodium: 150mg
- Total Carbohydrates: 29g
- Dietary Fiber: 1g
- Sugars: 5g
- Protein: 4g

Indulge in the delightful blend of cranberry, orange, and cinnamon with every slice of this aromatic and flavorful bread. Your kitchen will be filled with the enticing scent of freshly baked goodness, making this recipe a standout in your bread machine repertoire.

97. Asiago and Black Pepper Boule

Indulge in the savory delight of our Asiago and Black Pepper Boule, a bread machine creation inspired by the culinary genius of Gordon Ramsay. This artisanal loaf combines the nutty richness of Asiago cheese with the bold kick of black pepper, resulting in a bread that is both sophisticated and comforting. Elevate your bread-making skills with this flavorful masterpiece that's perfect for any occasion.

Serving: Yields one delicious boule, approximately 10 slices.
Preparation Time: 15 minutes
Ready Time: 3 hours (including rising and baking time)

Ingredients:
- 1 cup warm water (110°F/43°C)
- 2 tablespoons olive oil
- 1 teaspoon sugar
- 1 1/2 teaspoons salt
- 3 cups bread flour
- 1 teaspoon black pepper, freshly ground
- 1 cup Asiago cheese, shredded
- 2 teaspoons active dry yeast

Instructions:
1. Prepare the Bread Machine:
Place the warm water, olive oil, sugar, and salt in the bread machine pan.
2. Add Dry Ingredients:
Add the bread flour, black pepper, and shredded Asiago cheese on top of the wet ingredients in the pan.
3. Create a Well:
Make a small well in the center of the flour mixture without reaching the liquid.
4. Add Yeast:
Sprinkle the active dry yeast into the well.
5. Start the Machine:
Insert the pan into the bread machine and select the "Dough" cycle. Start the machine.

6. Monitor the Dough:
Keep an eye on the dough during the mixing and rising stages. If it appears too sticky, add a little more flour. If it's too dry, add a tablespoon of water.

7. Remove the Dough:
Once the dough cycle is complete, remove the dough from the machine and place it on a floured surface.

8. Shape the Boule:
Shape the dough into a round boule and place it on a parchment paper-lined baking sheet.

9. Final Rise:
Allow the dough to rise in a warm place for about 1 hour, or until it has doubled in size.

10. Preheat the Oven:
Preheat the oven to 375°F (190°C).

11. Bake:
Bake the boule for 25-30 minutes, or until it is golden brown and sounds hollow when tapped on the bottom.

12. Cool:
Allow the Asiago and Black Pepper Boule to cool on a wire rack before slicing.

Nutrition Information:
(per slice, assuming 10 slices)
- Calories: 180
- Total Fat: 6g
- Saturated Fat: 2.5g
- Cholesterol: 10mg
- Sodium: 350mg
- Total Carbohydrates: 25g
- Dietary Fiber: 1g
- Sugars: 1g
- Protein: 6g

Indulge in the delectable aroma and flavor of this bread, and let the combination of Asiago and black pepper take your taste buds on a culinary journey. Enjoy your homemade creation inspired by the one and only Gordon Ramsay.

98. Sunflower Seed Rye Bagels

Sunflower Seed Rye Bagels are a delightful fusion of traditional bagels and earthy rye flavors, topped with nutty sunflower seeds for an extra crunch. Inspired by Gordon Ramsay's flair for combining textures and tastes, these bagels will elevate your breakfast or brunch experience.

Serving: Makes 8 bagels
Preparation Time: 15 minutes
Ready Time: Approximately 2 hours 30 minutes

Ingredients:
- 1 cup warm water
- 2 tablespoons honey
- 2 ½ teaspoons active dry yeast
- 2 cups bread flour
- 1 cup rye flour
- 1 teaspoon salt
- 1 egg (for egg wash)
- ¼ cup sunflower seeds

Instructions:
1. Prepare the Dough:
- In the bread machine pan, combine the warm water and honey. Sprinkle the yeast over the mixture and let it sit for about 5 minutes until foamy.
- Add the bread flour, rye flour, and salt to the pan. Place the pan in the bread machine and select the dough setting. Start the machine.
2. Shape the Bagels:
- Once the dough cycle is complete, remove the dough from the machine and punch it down gently on a floured surface.
- Divide the dough into 8 equal portions and shape each into a ball. Using your finger, poke a hole through the center of each ball and gently stretch the hole to create the bagel shape. Ensure the hole is about 1 to 2 inches in diameter.
3. Rise and Boil:
- Preheat your oven to 400°F (200°C). Let the shaped bagels rise on a parchment-lined baking sheet for about 20-30 minutes, covered with a clean kitchen towel.

- Bring a large pot of water to a boil. Once the bagels have risen, carefully drop them, one or two at a time, into the boiling water. Boil each side for about 1-2 minutes, then remove them with a slotted spoon and place them back on the baking sheet.

4. Bake:
- Beat the egg and brush the tops of the bagels with the egg wash. Sprinkle sunflower seeds on top of each bagel.
- Bake the bagels in the preheated oven for 20-25 minutes or until they turn golden brown and sound hollow when tapped on the bottom. Transfer to a wire rack to cool.

Nutrition Information (per bagel, approximate):
- Calories: 220
- Total Fat: 3.5g
- Saturated Fat: 0.5g
- Cholesterol: 23mg
- Sodium: 300mg
- Total Carbohydrate: 40g
- Dietary Fiber: 3g
- Sugars: 5g
- Protein: 7g

Enjoy these Sunflower Seed Rye Bagels warm or toasted, with your favorite spreads or as a base for delicious sandwiches!

99. Lemon Thyme Olive Oil Bread

Lemon Thyme Olive Oil Bread is a delightful blend of citrusy zest, aromatic thyme, and the rich flavor of olive oil. Inspired by Gordon Ramsay's love for bold and fresh flavors, this bread machine recipe promises a harmonious balance of tangy and herbal notes in every slice.

Serving: 8-10 slices
Preparation Time: 15 minutes
Ready Time: 3 hours

Ingredients:
- 1 cup warm water

- 3 tablespoons olive oil
- Zest of 1 lemon
- 1 tablespoon fresh thyme leaves, chopped
- 3 cups bread flour
- 2 tablespoons sugar
- 1 teaspoon salt
- 2 teaspoons active dry yeast

Instructions:
1. Preparation: Start by greasing the bread machine pan lightly to prevent sticking.
2. Combine Wet Ingredients: In a mixing bowl, whisk together warm water, olive oil, lemon zest, and chopped thyme.
3. Combine Dry Ingredients: In a separate bowl, mix bread flour, sugar, and salt.
4. Assemble in Bread Machine: Pour the wet mixture into the bread machine pan. Add the dry ingredients on top. Make a small well in the center of the flour mixture and add the yeast.
5. Select Setting: Set your bread machine to the "Basic" or "White Bread" setting, according to the manufacturer's instructions.
6. Start Machine: Start the machine and let it run through the complete cycle.
7. Cool and Serve: Once the baking cycle is complete, carefully remove the bread from the pan and transfer it to a wire rack to cool for at least 30 minutes before slicing.

Nutrition Information (per slice, serving 8):
- Calories: 190
- Total Fat: 5g
- Saturated Fat: 1g
- Cholesterol: 0mg
- Sodium: 290mg
- Total Carbohydrates: 31g
- Dietary Fiber: 1g
- Sugars: 2g
- Protein: 5g

This Lemon Thyme Olive Oil Bread pairs wonderfully with soups, salads, or simply enjoyed on its own. Its refreshing flavors make it a delightful addition to any meal or a tasty snack for any time of the day.

100. Cheddar Bacon Beer Bread

Indulge in the savory goodness of Cheddar Bacon Beer Bread! This recipe draws inspiration from the bold flavors favored by Gordon Ramsay, combining the richness of cheddar, the smokiness of bacon, and the depth of beer in a delightful bread that's perfect for any occasion. Using a bread machine simplifies the process, ensuring a fuss-free, delectable result.

Serving: This recipe yields one loaf, approximately 12 slices.
Preparation Time: 10 minutes
Ready Time: 3 hours (including baking time)

Ingredients:
- 3 cups all-purpose flour
- 1 tablespoon baking powder
- 1 teaspoon salt
- ¼ cup granulated sugar
- 1 ½ cups grated sharp cheddar cheese
- 6 slices cooked bacon, crumbled
- 1 (12-ounce) bottle of beer, preferably a lager or ale
- ¼ cup unsalted butter, melted

Instructions:
1. Begin by setting up your bread machine with the kneading paddle attachment.
2. In the bread pan, combine the all-purpose flour, baking powder, salt, and sugar.
3. Add the grated cheddar cheese and crumbled bacon into the bread pan, mixing them with the dry ingredients.
4. Pour the bottle of beer over the mixture in the bread pan.
5. Place the bread pan into the bread machine and select the appropriate setting for a basic or white bread, ensuring a medium crust. Start the machine.
6. As the ingredients combine, allow the bread machine to knead the dough thoroughly.

7. Once the initial mixing is complete, open the lid and scrape down any flour or cheese that may be sticking to the sides of the bread pan, ensuring all ingredients are incorporated.

8. Close the lid and allow the bread machine to continue its cycle, letting the dough rise and bake.

9. When the baking cycle is complete, carefully remove the bread pan from the machine and place it on a wire rack to cool for a few minutes.

10. Brush the top of the bread with melted butter for added flavor and a glossy finish.

11. Let the bread cool in the pan for an additional 10 minutes before removing it from the pan and transferring it to the wire rack to cool completely.

Nutrition Information (per slice, approximately):
Calories: 240
Total Fat: 10g
Saturated Fat: 6g
Cholesterol: 30mg
Sodium: 480mg
Total Carbohydrate: 27g
Dietary Fiber: 1g
Total Sugars: 4g
Protein: 9g

Enjoy this Cheddar Bacon Beer Bread warm or toasted, and revel in its delightful blend of flavors that elevate any meal or make a perfect standalone treat.

101. Rosemary Sea Salt Fougasse

Elevate your bread machine repertoire with this delectable Rosemary Sea Salt Fougasse, a delightful creation inspired by the culinary genius of Gordon Ramsay. The aromatic blend of fresh rosemary and the subtle crunch of sea salt will transport your taste buds to a rustic French countryside. This bread is not only a feast for the senses but also a testament to the ease and excellence that can be achieved with your trusty bread machine.

Serving: Makes one large fougasse, approximately 8 servings.

Preparation Time: 15 minutes
Ready Time: 2 hours (including rise time)

Ingredients:
- 1 cup warm water (110°F/43°C)
- 2 teaspoons sugar
- 1 1/2 teaspoons active dry yeast
- 3 cups all-purpose flour
- 1 teaspoon salt
- 2 tablespoons olive oil
- 2 tablespoons fresh rosemary, finely chopped
- 1 teaspoon sea salt flakes

Instructions:
1. In a small bowl, combine warm water and sugar. Stir until the sugar dissolves. Sprinkle the yeast over the water and let it sit for 5-10 minutes, or until it becomes frothy.
2. In the bread machine pan, combine the flour, salt, and olive oil. Pour in the activated yeast mixture.
3. Set your bread machine to the dough setting and let it run its cycle. This typically takes about 1 to 1.5 hours, allowing the machine to knead and rise the dough.
4. Preheat your oven to 400°F (200°C).
5. Once the dough cycle is complete, transfer the dough to a floured surface. Roll it out into a large oval shape, about 1/2 inch thick.
6. Using a sharp knife, make several diagonal cuts on both sides of the oval, leaving the center intact. This will give your fougasse its characteristic leaf-like shape.
7. Carefully transfer the fougasse to a baking sheet lined with parchment paper.
8. Sprinkle the chopped rosemary over the top of the dough, and finish by sprinkling sea salt flakes evenly.
9. Bake in the preheated oven for 18-20 minutes or until the fougasse is golden brown and sounds hollow when tapped on the bottom.
10. Allow it to cool for a few minutes before slicing. Serve warm and enjoy the aroma and flavors of this Gordon Ramsay-inspired Rosemary Sea Salt Fougasse.

Nutrition Information:
(Per serving)

- Calories: 180
- Total Fat: 4g
- Saturated Fat: 0.5g
- Cholesterol: 0mg
- Sodium: 400mg
- Total Carbohydrates: 32g
- Dietary Fiber: 2g
- Sugars: 0.5g
- Protein: 4g

Note: Nutrition information is approximate and may vary based on specific ingredients used.

102. Hazelnut Chocolate Swirl Brioche

Indulge your senses in the exquisite world of artisanal bread-making with this Hazelnut Chocolate Swirl Brioche, a delightful creation inspired by the culinary genius of Gordon Ramsay. Elevate your baking experience with the perfect blend of rich hazelnuts and decadent chocolate, beautifully swirled into a soft and pillowy brioche. Whether you're a novice or a seasoned baker, this recipe promises a taste of luxury that will leave everyone craving for more.

Serving: Yields 1 Hazelnut Chocolate Swirl Brioche loaf, approximately 12 slices.
Preparation Time: 20 minutes
Ready Time: 3 hours (including rising and baking time)

Ingredients:
- 1 cup warm milk (110°F/43°C)
- 1/4 cup granulated sugar
- 2 1/4 teaspoons (1 packet) active dry yeast
- 4 cups all-purpose flour
- 1/2 teaspoon salt
- 3 large eggs
- 1/2 cup unsalted butter, softened
- 1/2 cup hazelnuts, finely chopped
- 1/2 cup chocolate chips or chopped chocolate
- 1/4 cup cocoa powder

- 1/4 cup brown sugar

Instructions:
1. In a bowl, combine warm milk and sugar. Sprinkle yeast over the mixture, let it sit for 5 minutes until frothy.
2. In a large mixing bowl, combine flour and salt. Make a well in the center and add the yeast mixture, eggs, and softened butter. Mix until a dough forms.
3. Knead the dough on a floured surface until smooth and elastic. Place the dough in a greased bowl, cover with a damp cloth, and let it rise in a warm place for 1-1.5 hours, or until doubled in size.
4. Punch down the risen dough and roll it out into a rectangle on a floured surface.
5. In a small bowl, mix together hazelnuts, chocolate, cocoa powder, and brown sugar. Spread this mixture evenly over the rolled-out dough.
6. Roll the dough tightly from one of the longer sides, forming a log. Place the log in a greased loaf pan.
7. Cover the pan with a damp cloth and let it rise for another 1-1.5 hours, or until it reaches the top of the pan.
8. Preheat your oven to 350°F (175°C). Bake the brioche for 25-30 minutes or until golden brown.
9. Allow the brioche to cool in the pan for 10 minutes before transferring it to a wire rack to cool completely.

Nutrition Information:
(per slice, based on 12 slices)
- Calories: 280
- Total Fat: 13g
- Saturated Fat: 6g
- Cholesterol: 65mg
- Sodium: 120mg
- Total Carbohydrates: 35g
- Dietary Fiber: 2g
- Sugars: 9g
- Protein: 6g

Enjoy this Hazelnut Chocolate Swirl Brioche as a luxurious treat for breakfast, brunch, or any time you want to savor a slice of perfection.

103. Pesto Sun-dried Tomato Ciabatta

Elevate your bread machine repertoire with this delightful Pesto Sun-dried Tomato Ciabatta recipe, inspired by the culinary genius of Gordon Ramsay. The perfect blend of Mediterranean flavors, this bread boasts the rich essence of sun-dried tomatoes and the vibrant kick of homemade pesto. Baked to perfection in your bread machine, this ciabatta is an irresistible combination of rustic charm and gourmet indulgence.

Serving: Makes approximately 1 large ciabatta loaf
Preparation Time: 15 minutes
Ready Time: 2 hours (including rising and baking time)

Ingredients:
- 1 cup warm water
- 2 tablespoons olive oil
- 3 cups bread flour
- 1 teaspoon sugar
- 1 1/2 teaspoons salt
- 1 tablespoon dry milk powder
- 2 teaspoons active dry yeast

For the Pesto:
- 1 cup fresh basil leaves, packed
- 1/2 cup grated Parmesan cheese
- 1/3 cup pine nuts
- 2 cloves garlic, peeled
- 1/2 cup extra-virgin olive oil
- Salt and pepper to taste

For the Filling:
- 1/2 cup sun-dried tomatoes, drained and chopped

Instructions:
1. Prepare the Pesto:
- In a food processor, combine basil, Parmesan cheese, pine nuts, and garlic.
- Pulse until finely chopped.
- With the processor running, gradually add olive oil until the pesto reaches a smooth consistency.
- Season with salt and pepper to taste. Set aside.

2. Bread Machine Preparation:
- In the bread machine pan, combine warm water, olive oil, bread flour, sugar, salt, and dry milk powder.
- Make a well in the center and add the yeast.
- Set the bread machine to the dough cycle and let it run.

3. Assemble the Dough:
- Once the dough cycle is complete, turn the dough out onto a floured surface.
- Roll the dough into a rectangle and spread the prepared pesto evenly over the surface.
- Sprinkle the chopped sun-dried tomatoes over the pesto.

4. Shape and Rise:
- Roll the dough into a log and place it seam side down on a parchment-lined baking sheet.
- Cover with a clean kitchen towel and let it rise in a warm place for about 30-45 minutes, or until doubled in size.

5. Bake:
- Preheat the oven to 375°F (190°C).
- Bake the ciabatta in the preheated oven for 25-30 minutes or until golden brown.
- Allow it to cool on a wire rack before slicing.

Nutrition Information:
(Per serving, based on 12 slices)
- Calories: 210
- Total Fat: 11g
- Saturated Fat: 2g
- Trans Fat: 0g
- Cholesterol: 3mg
- Sodium: 321mg
- Total Carbohydrates: 23g
- Dietary Fiber: 2g
- Sugars: 1g
- Protein: 5g

Indulge in the artisanal delight of this Pesto Sun-dried Tomato Ciabatta – a creation that seamlessly blends the expertise of your bread machine with the culinary inspiration of Gordon Ramsay.

CONCLUSION

Breaking Bread with Gordon Ramsay's Culinary Canvas

As we conclude this culinary journey through "Bread Bliss: 103 Inspired Recipes from Gordon Ramsay's Culinary Canvas," I can't help but reflect on the sheer joy and passion that the world-renowned chef has brought to the realm of cooking. Gordon Ramsay's influence extends far beyond the confines of the kitchen; it's a force that inspires, challenges, and elevates our approach to gastronomy. This cookbook, born out of admiration for his culinary prowess, is a humble tribute to the maestro himself, celebrating the art of bread-making that has left an indelible mark on our taste buds.

Each page of this cookbook is a testament to the diverse and innovative ways in which Gordon Ramsay approaches the world of flavors, textures, and aromas. The 103 bread machine recipes encapsulate the essence of his cooking style, seamlessly blending his signature techniques with the convenience of modern kitchen appliances. The goal was not merely to replicate his creations but to craft a collection that echoes his spirit—an amalgamation of boldness, creativity, and, above all, an unwavering commitment to quality.

The journey began with the desire to unravel the mysteries of bread-making, exploring the intricate dance of ingredients that transforms humble dough into a symphony of tastes. Inspired by Gordon Ramsay's relentless pursuit of perfection, each recipe in this collection is a carefully curated masterpiece, inviting both seasoned bakers and novices alike to embark on a delicious adventure. From the comforting warmth of classic loaves to the daring twists of artisanal breads, "Bread Bliss" beckons you to discover the joy of crafting your own culinary symphony.

While Ramsay may not have directly penned these pages, his influence is woven into the fabric of every recipe. The focus on fresh, high-quality ingredients, the meticulous attention to detail, and the unapologetic celebration of bold flavors—all pay homage to the culinary philosophy that Ramsay has championed throughout his illustrious career. In this cookbook, I have endeavored to channel his essence, providing you with a guide to recreate the magic of his kitchen in the comfort of your own home.

As you embark on your bread-making odyssey, remember that this cookbook is not just a collection of recipes; it's an invitation to embrace the joy of creation, to experiment fearlessly, and to savor the fruits of your labor. Gordon Ramsay's culinary journey has been marked by resilience, innovation, and an unyielding commitment to excellence. Let this cookbook be a source of inspiration as you continue to hone your skills, pushing the boundaries of what's possible in your own kitchen.

In closing, "Bread Bliss" is more than a cookbook; it's a celebration of the shared love for good food, the joy of experimentation, and the belief that anyone can create culinary masterpieces with the right guidance. May these 103 inspired recipes fill your home with the irresistible aroma of freshly baked bread, and may each bite transport you to the extraordinary world of flavors that Gordon Ramsay has so graciously shared with us all. Happy baking!

Made in the USA
Coppell, TX
14 March 2025